1599: Empires of Blood

Written by:
William Mowat

CROWN & ANCHOR PUBLISHING

—William Mowat—

—1599: Empires of Blood—

CROWN & ANCHOR PUBLISHING

crownandanchorpublishing@gmail.com

Copyright © 2025, William Mowat, Author
Published in Canada by Crown and Anchor Publishing,
Welland, Ontario L3B 3H9
ISBN 978-1-7380796-9-8

First Paperback Edition in 2025.

This is a historical work of fiction. Most characters, places, and incidents are products of the author's imagination, except for those that are historical or public, and are used fictitiously and are not to be construed as real. Any resemblance to actual events, locales, organizations, or persons, living or dead, is entirely coincidental.

All rights reserved. No part of this book may be used or reproduced in any manner without written permission, except in the case of brief quotations embodied in critical articles and reviews.

Any members of educational institutions or businesses wishing to copy part or all of the work for production use or would like to obtain permission to include work in an anthology should send their inquiries to: crownandanchorpublishing@gmail.com.

—William Mowat—

—1599: Empires of Blood—

"Beware of seeking fame and fortune in the belly of the beast."

—William Mowat—

Preface

Real events inspire the following story, though time has transformed much of it into legend. Facts have eroded into folklore, and historical truths have been cloaked in myth's shadows. This narrative exists in the space between what was and what might have been, where memory, imagination, and history intertwine.

A great upheaval was taking place as the medieval world gave way to the dawn of the Renaissance; shifting away from countries built upon divine right and unchecked authority, the rise of knowledge surged like a tide, crashing through the barriers of superstition and fear.

Truth emerged from the shadows as a period of profound cultural, artistic, and intellectual transformation took place in Europe between the late 14th and 17th centuries, marking the transition from the Middle Ages to modernity.

Originating in Italy, the Renaissance spread throughout Europe, leading to a resurgence of interest in classical antiquity and advancements in art, science, literature, and philosophy. In neighbouring England, the Renaissance arrived somewhat later, flourishing mainly in the 16th and early 17th centuries, with its height during the Elizabethan Age. The movement in England also coincided with significant religious and political changes, including the Reformation and the rise of Protestantism, shaping a unique national character for the English Renaissance.

The age of witchcraft and sorcery slowly gave way to empiricism and inquiry. Ships ruled the seas, and cannons and gunpowder were the determining factors on battlefields; the global commercial network was spreading, faintly, but irreversibly. William Shakespeare was reshaping language in the arts realm, offering humanity new ways to understand its soul and personal experience. Copernicus discovered that the Earth was not the universe's centre but a speck of stardust in a seemingly infinite galaxy. Truth and Science were now the guiding lights of society, rather than the ancient gods and traditions of yesterday.

And so, in 1599 AD, a moment suspended between the ancient and the modern. Blood still flows freely in the name of power. Thrones tremble. Empires teeter on the edge of collapse. And yet, within the chaos, something extraordinary is stirring: a new world struggling to be born. Welcome to the twilight of one age and the violent birth of another.

Cast of Main Characters

Peter Dowling - English teacher
Margaret Dowling - Peter's daughter
John Smith - Young English Soldier

Countess Elizabeth Bathory - Countess of Hungary
Count Ferenc Nadasdy - Husband to Elizabeth and Black Knight of Hungary
Count George Thurzo - Cousin of Elizabeth Bathory
Dorka, Helena, Illona, Fitzko - Servants to Elizabeth and Ferenc

Holy Roman Emperor Rudolph II - Holy Roman Emperor
Archduke Matthias - Rudolph's brother
The Earl of Meldritch - Transylvanian military leader

Maria Kovacs - Musician in the Village of Cachtice
Sam Kovacs - Younger brother of Maria
Jan and Catharine Kovacs - Parents of Maria and Sam
Michael Gorzi - Young Cachtice farmer
Pastor Istivan - Christian Clergyman in the Village of Cachtice

—William Mowat—

—1599: Empires of Blood—

Table of Contents

PROLOGUE 299 AD: THE DRAGON IS BORN_____15

CHAPTER 1 - THE DOWLINGS OF LONDON_____33

CHAPTER 2 - THE ORDER OF THE DRAGON_____39

CHAPTER 3 - THE BRITAINE'S NEW MAN_____49

CHAPTER 4 - BEWARE THE IDES OF MARCH_____57

CHAPTER 5 - THE HOLY ROMAN EMPIRE_____63

CHAPTER 6 - THE SCARLET SECRET_____69

CHAPTER 7 - WHISPERS TO A WILD HEART_____77

CHAPTER 8 - QUICKLY'S CHARM_____83

CHAPTER 9 - THE COUNT'S RETURN_____87

CHAPTER 10 - THE SHEPPARD AND HIS FLOCK_____93

CHAPTER 11 - A GRAND TOUR_____99

CHAPTER 12 - A TALE OF YOUTH_____109

CHAPTER 13 - THE THREE TURKS_____115

CHAPTER 14 - THE TUTOR ARRIVES_____123

CHAPTER 15 - ST. GEORGE'S SONGBIRD_____131

CHAPTER 16 - ROTHENTHRUM_____139

CHAPTER 17 - THE RED VEIL	**145**
CHAPTER 18 - CHARATZA	**153**
CHAPTER 19 - A TRANSITION OF POWER	**159**
CHAPTER 20 - A PORCELAIN MASK	**165**
CHAPTER 21 - THE THRESHING FLOOR	**171**
CHAPTER 22 - A CRIMSON PURCHASE	**175**
CHAPTER 23 - THE GYNAECEUM	**183**
CHAPTER 24 - A HOLY PLEA	**191**
CHAPTER 25 - THE SILK ROAD	**195**
CHAPTER 26 - WHERE SHADOWS DARE TO RUN	**207**
CHAPTER 27 - A GIFT FROM ABOVE	**213**
CHAPTER 28 - VENICE	**221**
CHAPTER 29 – A DEEP SCAR	**227**
CHAPTER 30 - THE SAINT GEORGE	**231**
CHAPTER 31 - SILENCE IN CACHTICE	**233**
CHAPTER 32 - THE MAN OF WAR	**237**
CHAPTER 33 - A GRANDIOSE FEAST	**243**
CHAPTER 34 - ALONG THE THAMES	**247**
CHAPTER 35 - A CELEBRATION OF VICTORY	**253**

CHAPTER 36 - A NEW WORLD PROJECT _____ **257**

CHAPTER 37 - 1608 _____ **261**

CHAPTER 38 - RETURN HOME _____ **271**

CHAPTER 39 - THE TRIAL _____ **275**

CHAPTER 40 - CONFRONTATION _____ **283**

CHAPTER 41 - THE TEMPEST _____ **287**

EPILOGUE _____ **291**

—William Mowat—

―1599: Empires of Blood―

Prologue 299 AD: The Dragon is Born

A bloodthirsty dragon emerged in the dark depths below the Earth's crust. Dimly lit from the smouldering lava within and the pale moon above, the beast carefully crawled up along the jagged rock walls. The talons of the long, sleek dragon sank into the crevice walls, sending fragments of quartz, limestone, and shale into the depths below. The beast's smoky breath vented from its nostrils and moved downward along its chest, sliding past its tail with each monstrous exhale. Its razor-sharp teeth oozed with salivation for a meal yet to come. Its eyes, black like the midnight sky, reflected only the moon as it approached the top of Earth's fracture.

Like being born from the earth's crust, the dragon emerged and spread its massive wings, stretching with a grumbling vibration that could be heard in the valleys below. Rocks shook loose as the beast moved its gaze around in its new, dark surroundings. Its reptilian-like movement was slow, deliberate, and maniacal in its posture and gaze. It turned its long neck, aligning its scales in perfect symmetry. It peered down to the dimly lit village below and contemplated its next move.

The year was 299 AD, and the Roman Empire had been split into four quarters after the great Tetrarchy. The two junior Caesars, Galerius and Constantius, were appointed to assist in governance. At the same time, Maximian would rule the Western Roman Empire, and Diocletian, a battle-hardened general, would rule the East. After nearly a decade of the new government order, cultures began to shift, and new decrees would arise.

Diocletian, the Eastern Roman Emperor, had spent a decade at war with Egypt, the Sarmatians, and, most recently, with Persia. Year after year of bloody war had led to a lasting peace where the borders of the Roman Empire were relatively secure, and bureaucracy could take hold and rule the day.

After the Roman-Persian wars, Emperor Diocletian returned to the great city of Antioch, the third-largest city in the Roman Empire, behind Rome and Alexandria. Antioch was founded on the Silk Road and became a major trade centre during the rise of the great Mediterranean culture.

Massive walls surrounded and fortified a bustling metropolis of Greek, Roman, and eastern cultures, as well as a growing Christian population. The town now included the massive Circus of Antioch, an 80,000-seat hippodrome to house the great chariot races of the day; it had temples and baths, aqueducts, markets, theatres, and various churches.

Christianity was steadily gaining momentum and influence throughout the vast expanse of the empire, reshaping cultural and spiritual landscapes in profound ways. Meanwhile, imperial edicts and soothsayers used ancient traditions of sacrifice to seek out signs and omens, hoping to decipher what the future might hold amid the tides of change.

Emperor Diocletian and Caesar Galerius sat awaiting the haruspex, the old soothsayer who performed various rituals and sacrifices upon the temple's altar. A young, ambitious Caesar Galerius sat, gleefully anticipating the coming spectacle. Emperor Diocletian, more a realist and diplomat than Galerius, was weary of the religious ceremonies and traditions of the haruspex. He knew the world was complex, barbaric, brutal, and constantly changing.

The old, robed haruspex emerged on the cold stone steps, pulling along a single, white goat. He tied off the animal and began preparing the altar. The haruspex cleaned the surface carefully and methodically decorated it with candles and silk cloth. As the old man prepared the altar, 12 priests entered the temple in single file and aligned themselves in pageantry around the altar.

The Latin prayers began as Galerius turned to Diocletian and smiled.

"Apollo, forever the son of Jupiter, of wise divinity, hear our prayers and guide our insight today. Grant us the vision of truth in these entrails we provide you. Oh, God of light, God of prophecy, our hearts and souls favour you and your divine will. Apollo, bring knowledge and healing to our world. This Christian uprising contests your almighty wisdom," the haruspex said, raising his old, bony hands in the air.

The prayers were not convincing to Diocletian, who impatiently thought of all his men sacrificing themselves on the gruesome battlefields throughout the past decade. This goat almost seemed foolish to him. Why hadn't Apollo shown his divinity on the plains of Persia or the deserts of Egypt?

"Jupiter, ruler of the heavens, and Mars, ruler and fierce protector of Rome, by your authority, we seek protection. We stand here and await your guidance with obedience and devoted favour."

The goat was then guided onto the altar and stood unknowingly and clueless about what was coming. The haruspex removed a blade from his sheath and slit the neck of the unsuspecting animal. The goat gurgled its last breath and fell limp to its knees. Two of the closest priests to the altar brought forth a pair of wooden bowls and collected the blood as the animal keeled over in death.

"Here comes the incision," Galerius whispered to Diocletian.

The haruspex sliced along the ribcage of the goat as the entrails spilt onto the altar. The priests carried the wooden bowls away as the haruspex raised his arms.

"Show us Apollo, Jupiter, Mars, show us the future of our empire," the haruspex said, looking to the heavens.

The haruspex examined the liver first, hunching over the altar to check the size and colour of the organ. He inspected for any abnormalities or defects. His urgency and determined focus showed his fear of what could be a sign that the gods were upset or displeased.

Blood poured over the altar, as the soothsayer continued to examine the heart, kidneys and intestines. He paid no worry to the blood that was now covering the front of his robe and hands. Diocletian and Galerius looked on with curious anticipation.

Suddenly, the haruspex stepped back, startled by the sight of something irregular. His eyes widened, and he covered his mouth with the sleeve of his robe. "I am unable to read the entrails," the haruspex announced. "The vile Christian faith clouds our ability to communicate with our Roman Gods."

Diocletian turned to Galerius. "Clouds our communication?" he asked sarcastically.

"The growing number of Christians within our imperial domain has broken the line of communication," Galerius responded, staring at the sacrifice.

"And what would the Gods have us do?" Diocletian hypothetically asked.

The haruspex turned to the two sitting emperors. "The Christ followers have silenced the voices of my Lords, Apollo, Jupiter, and Mars. These people follow a man being sacrificed for committing crimes and heresy against Jupiter and Apollo. The sickness must be cleansed," he said, bowing his head.

"Peculiar," Galerius said.

"Peculiar, indeed," Diocletian added, referring to the entire ceremonial sacrifice.

Two priests removed the blood-soaked corpse of the goat and carried it off on a large wooden platter. The organs were removed and placed in buckets by another priest, while another holy man carefully washed the altar with a sponge and water.

"We will dine tonight upon this goat and its holy sacrifice. With each bite, we must remind ourselves of our commitment to the mighty Apollo, Jupiter, and Mars. We hope to send a message to our Gods that we are still subservient to their divine wisdom in this communal feast, despite our ability to hear and communicate with them," the haruspex announced.

"We must maintain the pax deorum," Galerius said to Diocletian.

"Yes, pax deorum; peace with the Gods," the haruspex said in agreement.

"Certainly, peace with the Gods needs to be honoured, but we hear them not," Diocletian responded.

"Christianity clouds our Empire and is spreading like a rabid sickness," Galerius said. "Let us send a message to the military command. Let us begin the purge of Christians and their toxic religion from our holy Roman Empire." Galerius said, smiling, as his eyes gleamed with a sense of triumph. The young Emperor had long believed that the growth of the Christian faith threatened the unity and strength of Rome, and he felt a sense of vindication in his determination to rid the empire of what he saw as a destabilizing force.

Diocletian observed the unfolding turmoil with a calm yet uneasy resolve. Ever the pragmatist, he recognized that religious unity was crucial to preserving the fragile stability of the empire. Yet, he was keenly aware that the measures required to enforce this Christian eradication would be harsh and unrelenting in the months ahead.

Together, Diocletian and Galerius agreed to orchestrate a brutal campaign, one that would severely test the faith and devotion of countless Christians throughout the Empire, unleashing a wave of bloodshed and sacrifice unlike anything seen before.

The dark, sleek dragon flew along the valleys and mountains of Asia Minor and the far reaches of the Eastern Roman Empire. It soared silently for years, unnoticed in the shadowy clouds above. It watched as men killed each other on the battlefields of Asia and Europe. The dragon eventually tired and landed in a remote, stagnant swamp. After years of building hunger, the serpent slithered into the muddy waters in search of food.

The swamp was empty of prey, and the beast needed to search elsewhere. The dragon began his midnight hunting on nearby farms, looking for anything it could sink its talons into;

anything he could bring back to the dark swamp lands and feed upon.

The neighbouring village's people began to notice their animals' disappearance and began a midnight watch effort. Night after night, different men would carry swords and torches and carefully browse the neighbouring fields looking for any signs of the beast.

On the thirteenth night of the watch, the dragon finally appeared. Its colossal wings unfurled with a thunderous whoosh as it landed in the wheat pasture below. The watchman, stationed on the ridge, stood frozen in terror as he gripped his torch tightly.

The watchman's trembling fingers betrayed him, and his torch slipped from his grasp, plummeting into the muddy earth with a dull splash. Adrenaline and anxiety surged through his veins as he stood motionless. The dragon's eyes, gleaming with an ancient, almost knowing intelligence, locked onto the terrified watchman's fear and approached the helpless man.

As the beast approached, the farmhand drew a sword. The dragon carefully inspected the human and smelled the helpless, quivering man. Suddenly, the dragon clasped the man around the waist and flew off. The sword fell out of his hand and landed in the damp pastureland, as he let out a bellowing, fading scream.

Diocletian, leader of the Eastern Empire, and Galerius, Caesar of Rome, were surrounded by their aged military council, discussing the Christian problem within their ranks.

"If we purge the Christians from our military ranks and remove them from political office, we would have sent a significant message and could potentially open up our communication with the Gods," Diocletian said.

"This will not be significant enough, Diocletian. The Gods demand a different approach. We are hindered by our lack of communication with Apollo. We need to persecute these Christians," Galerius said. "We need to exterminate them. Wipe them from the earth."

"These are citizens of our Empire, and they only praise the Son of God, who was brutally crucified in Jerusalem," Diocletian rebutted.

"They are plaguing our society, Diocletian. We must burn their churches and scriptures, seize their assets, and loot their treasuries. We will execute their high priests and prove their God cannot save them," Galerius said, pounding his fist on the council table.

Diocletian was uneasy about Galerius and his intentions. The young Caesar had known nothing but the royal luxuries of the Roman court. Diocletian was more of a soldier's soldier. He had empathy for all people, especially considering the troublesome time they lived in.

"Let us hope that we can re-establish communication with Apollo," Diocletian said.

The dragon's appetite had grown insatiable, fueled by a newly discovered taste for human flesh and blood. Entire villages were reduced to smouldering ruins. The dragon unleashed devastating attacks with its breath of fire; hotter than any furnace or forge, capable of turning wooden homes and fields to ash within moments.

In a desperate hope to quell the creature's wrath, terrified villagers began offering sacrifices, helpless peasant girls chosen by cruel fate. On the outskirts of their settlements, they stripped the young women bare and bound them tightly to rough-hewn wooden stakes exposed to the cold night and the dragon's watchful glare. These offerings seemed to satisfy the beast for a fleeting time, delaying its fiery destruction.

With everything seemingly hopeless, word was sent to the military council of Antioch. In their message to Diocletian, they pleaded for reinforcements, for warriors or hunters capable of slaying the seemingly invincible terror that haunted their lands.

The edict against Christians had begun in 303 AD. Romans burned the churches, destroyed scriptures, and forbade worship. The hate and intolerance for Christians spread across the Roman Empire.

Roman armies marched through cities, taking what they wanted, burning anything they touched, and taking prisoners who still preached the word of Jesus Christ.

Diocletian sent one Roman division to the eastern reaches to investigate the dragon that was killing and demanding human sacrifices. When the Roman contingency arrived, they discovered the bleak impoverishment of entire villages. Scorched earth and rubble from fallen buildings were all that remained.

Diocletian had demanded information. He initially believed it might be the neighbouring Persians or Sarmatians from the North. Regardless, he needed answers.

The Roman commander that Diocletian had dispatched met with a local magistrate whose daughter had been taken by the dragon at night. The commander hardly believed it could have been a lone dragon to cause all the surrounding damage.

"The beast has taken my daughter to the black swamps. Its evil permeates these lands. Our animals are gone, crops destroyed, and citizens are dying. Please, commander, save my daughter and kill this dragon," the magistrate pleaded.

"We shall investigate these black swamps and try to find this dragon," the Roman commander answered.

The Roman commander organized a small cavalry contingency to head north to the black swamps and provide some reconnaissance. Meanwhile, the rest of the legion would construct a massive trap for the dragon.

The six mounted riders dispatched north. Through the forested creek-beds and rocky paths, the horsemen galloped with haste. Dark clouds covered the sky as the valleys flattened and the air thickened. The grim, ominous setting made the riders feel uneasy; their heads swivelled and scanned each movement and sound that came their way.

The lowlands were full of thick smog, which made breathing more difficult for the riders.

"I say we report what we've seen," the first rider said.

"Turn around now? We have not seen anything," the second rider said.

"We must keep moving until we find this dragon," the third rider said.

The next day of riding, the sky turned dark grey, and visibility was still low for the unsuspecting riders. The dragon soared silently and unsuspectingly above the Roman riders. The beast carefully observed the horsemen and finally began his aerial attack.

The first rider was snatched up by the powerful talons of the dragons and dropped from a thousand feet above the ground.

"Spread out!" a rider yelled.

The dragon's next pass, he blew a hundred-yard flame, cooking two riders to death.

The dragon methodically landed in front of the three remaining riders. The first one charged, and the dragon swallowed the poor rider whole, sword, shield, and all. The horse galloped away from the beast as fast as it could, and just as it thought it got away, the dragon took a swipe and cut the horse's hind legs off. The dragon let out a bellowing victory scream as the two remaining soldiers looked at one another in disbelief.

The two soldiers gathered their courage, nodded at one another, and charged the beast together, but the dragon plunged his talons through the chest of one rider and knocked the other off his horse.

The lone living soldier got up and composed himself, spear and shield in hand. The knight stood face-to-face with the imposing dragon as it stood on its hind legs. The beast raised its head and let out another terrible screech, almost deafening the lone soldier.

The knight saw an opportunity. He held his shield high and charged the giant beast. The dragon bent his neck down to see the charging knight. As the dragon opened his mouth, the brave soldier hurled the spear with all his might. The long, sharp, Roman spear lodged in the back of the dragon's throat, and he threw his neck in the air and let out a piercing cry.

The lone knight moved under the belly of the beast, as the dragon hacked at the small spear stuck in its throat. From under the dragon, the knight gained his breath and did his best to avoid contact, hiding from the serpent's eyes. He peered toward the swamp and, a hundred feet away, caught sight of the magistrate's naked daughter lying face down on the muddy edge of the swamp. He could not be sure if she was alive or dead, but he had to confront the dragon before checking on her welfare.

The dragon spun its head around, looking for the lost knight.

The brave knight drew his sharpened sword and took a deep breath under the dragon's belly. The soldier looked at his sword, which had served him well in many clashes with enemies. He then slashed at the Achilles heel of the dragon, and the beast let out another trumpeting roar. As the dragon bent its head to look under its belly, the knight swiftly moved around its rear and around to its side. The knight climbed a nearby boulder, jumped toward the unsuspecting dragon, and brought down his blade on the neck of the dragon with all his might. The sharp blade sliced through the neck of the beast and sent its giant head rolling on the dark, damp ground.

Knowing he had killed the beast, the knight threw down his sword, shield, and helmet and ran toward the magistrate's daughter. The knight rolled the young woman on her back and checked to see if she was breathing. She let out a small moan, and the knight smiled at the sign of life in the young woman.

The knight wrapped the girl in a blanket and picked her up. He carried her for days, out of the swamp and back to the village where the Roman legion awaited. The legion had built a complex trap with a pit and net; however, they realized it was all for naught when they saw the lone knight carrying the magistrate's daughter.

"A lone knight approaches!" a Roman sentry cried.

The Roman commander emerged from his tent to see the knight carrying the magistrate's daughter. "Alert the magistrate at once!"

"Yes, sir," the sentry answered.

"My God, he did it," the commander said to himself.

Later that night, as the Roman legion and townspeople celebrated the brave knight and his acts of bravery, the magistrate confronted the young knight. "Son, what you have done for my town and for my family will never be forgotten," the magistrate said.

"I was driven by faith. It was the glory of God that powered me. Christ bestowed the courage and strength to slay the dragon," the knight said. "Without him, I would have been powerless."

"The Christ God has made you brave and worthy of glory," the magistrate said. "What is your name, soldier?"

"George, sir," the humble knight said.

The Roman Empire remained in the midst of the war against Christians. Romans burned churches, Bibles, and scriptures, beheaded bishops, and boiled worshippers alive. They exiled some priests, stripped thousands of citizens of their rights and worth, and, in some cases, imprisoned or tortured Christians to death in chambers of horror.

Many Christians entered into lives of secrecy, and others turned against their fellow Christ-followers. Those in captivity who refused their faith would be executed in horrific ways. Many were fed to wild animals within arenas across the Roman Empire. Many Christians were burned alive, had their fingers and eyes removed, their skin peeled off, and brutally tortured if they refused to renounce their faith in Jesus.

In Lydda, south of Antioch, where George was born and raised, Diocletian welcomed his returning legion from the farthest reaches of Asia Minor. While somewhat skeptical of a dragon, especially one demanding human sacrifices, he was happy that they had returned in good spirits and large numbers.

The Roman commander relayed the extraordinary tale of George's bravery to Diocletian, and the moment in the swamp when he faced the mighty dragon that had terrorized the region. He told the story of his unwavering courage and skill, and how George had slain the fearsome beast, rescuing the young magistrate's daughter from certain death. But the commander's account went beyond mere heroism; he spoke with reverence of George's deep and unshakeable faith in Christ. It was this profound devotion, he explained, that had given George the strength and resolve to confront and overcome such an embodiment of evil.

When the story reached Diocletian's ears, he was initially uncertain. The idea of a single man empowered by faith to triumph over such a monstrous threat seemed almost too fantastical for the seasoned emperor. Yet, despite his doubts and contentment in the dragon's death, Diocletian ordered George's arrest and imprisoned him in the ancient city of Lydda. There, in a grim, shadowed torture chamber beneath cold stone walls, George was bound in heavy iron chains.

Determined to break the young warrior's Christian spirit, Diocletian personally visited the cell. He employed every tactic to bend George's will: stern threats, promises of clemency, and even lavish bribes. Diocletian dangled gold, land, and title, hoping to sway him from his faith. But George remained immovable, his devotion unshaken. He repeatedly refused to renounce Christ, his eyes shining with quiet strength and unwavering conviction. His steadfastness only deepened Diocletian's frustration, planting seeds of both admiration and unease within the emperor's heart.

After days of being chained, without food and water, George was sent to the torture rack, where his skin was torn with butcher hooks. His wounds were filled with salt and vinegar, yet he did not scream or cry, showing only the same bravery that helped him slay the evil dragon in Asia Minor.

George's torture continued by being stretched and beaten with wooden clubs. He was then placed in a box full of nails that pierced his skin and spilled even more blood than the butcher hooks. Eventually, the executioner pulled the weak George from the box.

"Do you renounce the faith of Jesus Christ?" the executioner asked.

"I still have three more deaths to endure," George answered.

The executioner was confused by his answer, but didn't hesitate to put George in a boiling cauldron of water. Despite the scalding temperatures, he didn't scream or show any signs of pain. When George was removed from the boiling water, his entire body was bloated with boils and blisters, and his eyes had swollen shut. Then, George's head was placed in a vice, and six-inch nails were driven into the tips of his fingers and the sides of his skull.

As George lay bleeding and on the brink of death, Diocletian ordered his personal magician to the torture chamber, where he gave George two cups of poison. The magician had concocted the elixir with the most toxic substances known and had witnessed it killing people within seconds. He saw George drink the two full cups and couldn't believe he was still alive. Hour after hour, George continued to breathe.

As the hours passed, George's chest still rose and fell with each breath. The magician watched in disbelief as the poison failed to claim its victim. Miraculously, George lived. Overcome with awe and conviction, the magician dropped to his knees and swore to forsake his dark ways and pledge himself to Christ, vowing never to return to the path of sorcery again.

Learning of the magician's conversion in faith and the poison not working, Diocletian took swift action and had the magician killed.

A furious Diocletian made his way down into the torture chamber, followed by his wife, Alexandra. They both saw the burnt, beaten, and severely wounded George lying in his cell, still breathing. His bleeding, bloated body shocked Diocletian and Alexandra, as they stared at the pools of blood surrounding his body. They stood before the cell door and watched what could only be a miracle.

"I knew your father, George," Diocletian said with a teary eye. "He would not want this for you. He would not want to see you in such intolerable pain. Just renounce this foolish Christ God, and you shall live."

"Please, George," Alexandra added, crying tears of her own. "Your Empire needs you."

George slowly turned his head toward the Emperor and his wife. "I am almost at the gates of Heaven, a paradise for eternity," the swollen-faced George said. "God is forever with me."

The crying Alexandra looked on with horror. "I denounce these Roman Gods and pledge my undying faith in you, George, and in God and his Son, Jesus Christ," she said, weeping.

"Travel well, George. Let us finish this," Diocletian said.

"So be it," George said.

Diocletian turned to the executioner and motioned for George's beheading. The next day, on April 23rd, the executioner sharpened his blade with careful attention and beheaded George. The executioner spiked his swollen head on the walls of Lydda for everyone to see.

The spiking of George's head, a gruesome act meant to crush Christian spirit and serve as a warning to all who defied the Emperor, did not have the effect that Diocletian had hoped. The Emperor anticipated that such a brutal display of power would extinguish the flame of resistance and intimidate the growing Christian movement.

Rather than breaking the will of the faithful, George's martyrdom ignited a fervour of devotion. Christians across the Empire saw his courage as a symbol of divine strength, not weakness. Instead of silencing his voice, it spread, and the message of his faith grew louder with each passing century.

—William Mowat—

Chapter 1 - The Dowlings of London

Thirteen centuries after the torture and execution of St. George, his legacy and his courage live on. Stories of his sacrifice, overcoming the odds, and defeating the evil dragon had survived the Middle Ages. In 1599, thirteen centuries after his death, England flies his red and white banner as a symbol of courage and faith.

The streets of London in 1599 were muddy and treacherous. It had been a summer with significant rain that left people walking along planks and make-shift walkways to avoid sinking a foot into the unforgiving mud.

London was a bustling city of a quarter of a million people, the centre for political and economic trade within England, and a major city in Europe. A decade earlier, Queen Elizabeth led a great naval victory against the Spanish Armada and Philip II, and now the English were in a position of power on the global stage. Merchants, craftsmen, traders, sailors, and artists crowded the narrow streets. Timber-framed houses, old stone buildings, and the remnants of medieval architecture made up the patchwork of London.

Because there were so few street names or numbers, signs hung from all buildings, including home residences. Crowns often represented inns or hotels, lions or bulls might represent taverns, keys might represent a locksmith, a rose would represent an apothecary, and a hanging coat of arms represented the family within.

Though there were certain classes of people within England, it was a far cry from what was happening in the far east in Hungary and Transylvania. The poor in England could still earn somewhat of a living, whereas in the east, peasants were treated like cattle or worse.

London had a bustling art scene in 1599, and the Globe Theatre was at the heart of it. This evening was Julius Caesar's premiere, and citizens lined up and down Park Street in anticipation of the historic tragedy. The eager audience, wealthy and poor, had witnessed Shakespearean plays for nearly a decade and were excited to see the action unfold on the Globe stage.

Peter Dowling and his teenage daughter Margaret were two of the eager audience members awaiting admission into the newly constructed Globe Theatre. Peter was a grammar school teacher on the south side of London, and Margaret had employment in a dressmaker's shop a few blocks from the small school where Peter taught.

Margaret's mother had tragically passed away after a complication during childbirth. Peter raised Margaret alone, with help from Peter's ailing mother and father, who were both now gone. Peter raised Margaret wholeheartedly, giving her an uncommon education for young girls in Elizabethan London. Peter taught her how to read at six, perform complex math problems by ten, and was now teaching her Greek and Latin in her early teenage years.

Peter and Margaret had also been watching plays together for years. They had watched plays at the Rose Theatre, the Swan Theatre, and the Hope Theatre, and now they were about to watch a play at the brand new, illustrious Globe Theatre, home of William Shakespeare and The Lord Chamberlain's Men.

"Father, from what I have gathered, Julius Caesar was a good and wise leader," Margaret said as they strolled. "I wonder how Shakespeare will present the leader. Will he present him as a wise leader or a tyrant who deserves his fate?" she philosophically asked.

"If there is one thing that Shakespeare has shown us, it is that every character is not as one-sided as we think. They are complex, flawed, waning, motivated, and layered," Peter answered.

"Books suggest someone killed Caesar out of jealousy, envy, and ambition," Margaret said.

"Shakespeare does like to reflect current society within his plays. I wonder if he sees the parallels between Caesar and our Queen Elizabeth," Peter suggested.

"Perhaps Shakespeare sees that, like Caesar, Elizabeth is aging and refuses to provide an heir to her kingdom, or empire in Caesar's case," Margaret responded.

"Interesting theory," Peter said with a proud smile. "I wonder."

As they chatted and waited for entrance into the massive theatre, Peter felt a gentle tap on his shoulder. He spun around to see a well-dressed, older man with a long goatee.

"Hello there," the man said with a German accent. "I am sorry to bother."

"Good afternoon, sir," Peter responded.

"I couldn't help but overhear your intelligent, introspective conversation. My name is Thomas Platter," he said, shaking hands with Peter and Margaret. "I am visiting merry England from Switzerland. Is this your first Shakespeare play?" he asked.

"Peter Dowling, it's a pleasure," the speculating father said. "Mr. Platter, we have seen many productions. Much Ado About Nothing, As You Like It, A Midsummer Night's Dream, Romeo and Juliet, just to name a few. The theatre is at the heart of London society." Peter said.

"You must be very well-educated," Platter assumed, smiling at Margaret.

"I am a grammar school teacher. I was at King Edward VI Grammar School in Louth for nearly a decade. I am currently teaching Greek and Latin, here within the city at Merchant Taylors' School," Peter said.

"Ah, terrific. That is what I assumed from the nature of your knowledgeable and engaging conversation. You and your daughter speak so astutely. I don't mean to impose, but I have spent a great while in Germany, Austria, Bohemia, and Hungary, and they are looking for all types of teachers, tutors, and professionals, and the royal court is willing to pay whatever the cost," Platter said. "King Rudolph is wealthy beyond imagination."

"Interesting," Peter responded.

"King Rudolph holds many titles, including the Holy Roman Emperor. His castle and court are filled with famous astronomers, alchemists, mathematicians, and distinguished linguists such as yourselves. I have spent several months in the Emperor's palace in Prague as a teacher of ancient antiquities. The Emperor's collection contains the most fascinating inventions, diverse machines, foreign contraptions, not to mention the finest art collection the world has ever seen."

"He must pay well if he can afford such an extravagant collection," Peter said.

"He has paintings by Di Vinci, Raphael, Titian, Tintoretto, and Paul Veronese. The Emperor has the teeth of mermaids, feathers of the phoenix, and the horns of unicorns. He has a precious gem collection like no other; emeralds, sapphires, pearls, and diamonds the size of my fist. He has halls dedicated to ancient armour, Greek weapons from the Peloponnesian War, and Egyptian antiquities predating Rameses, things the world has not yet seen. Rooms of gold and silver coins, medals, bronze figures, priceless vases, and marble statues done by the world's most talented artists," Platter said.

"That does sound alluring and most interesting," Peter said.

"Fascinating," Margaret added.

"His collection is so vast, he has built two separate buildings across from the church of St. George," Platter continued. "He employs the finest, wisest curators and librarians. Rudolph II has guarded this collection with all of his attention for years. Room after room, masterpiece after masterpiece. It is unlike any other collection in the history of the world."

"Mr. Platter, what would you predict that a tutor, such as myself, would make in the Royal Palace of Prague?" Peter asked, as he glanced at Margaret.

"At least ten times what they are paying you at grammar school. The Lords of the eastern reaches pay in pure gold. They are rich beyond your wildest dreams," Platter said. "Rudolph treats his royal court very well. He seldom leaves the palace, so he trusts his inner circle unconditionally."

Peter looked at Margaret in her muddy dress and smiled. "Who would I contact regarding a potential position and contract with the Emperor?" Peter sincerely asked Platter.

"Come by the Three Blackbirds Inn this evening, and I will provide you with the Emperor's secretary. Then you might create correspondence. I am honest when I say that many people have earned vast fortunes through their time at the Royal Palace. The Emperor believes highly in the Renaissance. He admires the astronomy of our universe, the voices of artists, and modern technology that continues to evolve." Platter said. "You will have no regrets should you choose to take a position in the Holy Roman Empire."

"An exciting proposition," Peter said, "Perhaps I shall stop by the Three Blackbirds this evening, around 7 pm?"

"That would be terrific, Mr. Dowling," Platter responded.

As the crowd began to rumble, Margaret's attention waned. Peter and Mr. Platter finished making arrangements as the doors of the new Globe Theatre opened and the crowd started to push their way in.

"Mr. Platter, I thank you. I sincerely hope you enjoy the show!" Peter said as the crowd pushed them in opposite directions.

"Thank you, good luck, Mr. Dowling!" Platter said. "See you later this evening!" he said, tipping his cap.

Chapter 2 - The Order of the Dragon

In the far reaches of eastern Europe, the noble Bathory family ruled the lands of Hungary. Long ago, they had adopted the St. George legacy, when it was permanently immortalized on their coat of arms. There were even stories of Bathory ancestors defeating dragons in Carpathia's dark, forested mountains.

A colourful, hand-carved Bathory coat of arms, featuring three dragon teeth, hung proudly in Elizabeth Bathory's master bedroom chamber at Castle Cachtice. Elizabeth was proud of the shield that immortalized St. George and his defeat of the dragon. She reflected on it daily, remembering biblical tales, family members, and the kingdom under her family's protection. As a member of the Order of the Dragon, the Bathory family had always idolized St. George and the triumph of good over evil for years.

The Order of the Dragon had been established in the Eastern Empire, uniting all of Christendom against their enemies, especially the Muslim Ottoman Empire, whom they had been fighting for centuries. Elizabeth had a long line of powerful relatives who flew the flag for the Order of the Dragon, including Vlad Dracul, her distant cousin, known for battling Mehmed II and impaling his enemies on spikes outside his castle walls.

Elizabeth was the most powerful woman in Hungary and Transylvania, and had been for years. She owned and operated castles, oversaw villages and farms, and ruled everything in between with an iron fist. Through hundreds of years of arranged marriages, she was at the head of a family that was second only to the Holy Roman Emperor Rudolph II.

Elizabeth was the Countess of the Order of the Dragon, which was modelled to defend the Pope and the Christian Kingdoms of Europe against the mighty Turkish armies of the Ottoman Empire, and any other surrounding enemies looking to destroy Christendom. For hundreds of years, the Order of the Dragon had successfully repelled the Ottomans; however, it was an ongoing strife that never seemed to end.

Life in Hungary was often brutal. Violence was everywhere, and Elizabeth had grown accustomed to its ruling practices, morbid traditions, and gruesome nature. Elizabeth, now 40 years old, ruled with dispassion and crude, unyielding ways. The Countess and her husband, Count Ferenc Nadasdy, were in charge of seven castles, 29 villages, and thousands of peasants, whom they treated as animals or worse.

Elizabeth was a prominent Bathory family member, consisting of barons, princes, palatines, dukes, and royal judges from around Eastern Europe. Elizabeth was born into royalty and had never known anything besides lavish ceremonies, grandiose feasts, and royal entertainments. She had never had an empty stomach, nor had to wait impatiently. She had never developed blisters on her hands or worn ragged clothes; she was a celebrity of the Carpathian Mountains, Hungary, and the Holy Roman Empire.

Elizabeth lay sleeping in the dull, grey afternoon at Castle Cachtice, the palace she had inherited at the time of her marriage. She tossed and turned in her lavish bed as sweat soaked through her nightgown. Throughout most of her life, Elizabeth experienced epileptic seizures, extreme fatigue, and night terrors. In her privileged childhood, she was expected to grow up quickly. Tutored by the best minds, she was taught courtly etiquette and learned how to keep servants obedient, often through ruthless violence.

Illona, one of Elizabeth's most trusted personal servants, knocked on the chamber door. She heard the moaning and commotion of Elizabeth's turbulent sleep and decided to enter.

"Miss Elizabeth!" Illona yelled as she approached the bedside.

Illona was an old, weathered, no-nonsense servant who had been at the side of the Bathory family since before Elizabeth was born. She was among the highest-ranking servants at Castle Cachtice and taught Elizabeth many ways to keep the peasant class fearful and obedient within her realm.

In an inaudible voice, Elizabeth moaned, "No, no, you can't do this to me!"

"Miss Elizabeth, your highness, awake now!" Illona said, gently grabbing Elizabeth's shoulder.

"Let me out of here!" Elizabeth said as her eyes opened and she saw Illona standing above her.

"A dream, your highness, a dream," Illona said in a comforting tone.

A ghostly pale, soaking wet Elizabeth looked around and got her bearings. "The dream, Illona, the dream was terrible. Confined, enslaved, made a prisoner."

"Just a nightmare, your Grace. Are you alright?" Illona asked. "Here, take some water."

Illona poured a small cup of water from a clay pitcher and handed it to Elizabeth. She sipped the small cup at the edge of her bed. Her hands trembled as she struggled to hold the cup and maintain her composure.

"My nerves, Illona."

"Yes, my Grace. Let us put this nightmare behind us." Illona was doing her best to console the clearly panicked Elizabeth.

"I saw my husband, Illona. His head was on the end of a spike. The hoard blamed me for his murder." Elizabeth rose from her bed and began to dress in her evening wear.

Elizabeth had not seen her husband, Ferenc, for months, which was not uncommon, as the Hungarians had been at war with the Ottoman Empire for seven years. Ferenc was never far from a battlefield throughout the period and was fiercely battling the Sultan Mehmed III along the Danube River, the natural geographic border between Hungary and the Turkish lands of the Ottoman Empire.

"I have come to see if you were awake, as a letter from Castle Sarvar has just arrived," Illona said.

"My dear Ferenc has found time to write," Elizabeth said, gathering her strength.

Castle Sarvar was another property owned by Elizabeth and Ferenc along the Danube River. For years, the castle had been a focal point, a battleground, and a critical stronghold between the Christian positions and the Turkish Muslims of eastern Asia.

Elizabeth knew the dangers of living at Castle Sarvar and was elated to receive a letter from her dear husband. Any letter was exciting, as they were too seldom and instantly indicated that Ferenc was still alive and well.

Elizabeth loved her husband dearly. Count Ferenc Nadasdy and Elizabeth were married in 1575 in front of almost 5000 guests. Their noble, distinguished marriage combined lands and wealth throughout Hungary and Transylvania and solidified who was in power in the area. Ferenc had given Elizabeth the Castle Cachtice and the surrounding 17 villages as a wedding gift.

Together they had raised three children, two daughters and one son within the castle. Tutored privately, their children were rarely seen within the castle. The two oldest girls had recently moved to Prague to study with private courtly tutors, just as Elizabeth did when she was young. Much was expected of their children, especially the youngest prince, Paul. Now five years old, he was tutored within Castle Cachtice, but in his teenage years, he would be tutored in the Holy court of the Roman Emperor, Rudolph II, in Prague.

The early years of the Nadasdy-Bathory marriage were blissful and full of magic as they ruled a relatively peaceful kingdom. They raised a family and travelled joyfully throughout Europe, but now, with the terrible ongoing war with the Turks around them, the magic was nearly gone, and blood and violence enveloped their world.

The violence and nature of the ongoing strife numbed the senses of nearly everyone in the area, including the iron fist of Count Ferenc Nadasdy. His military duty had left him void of empathy and thirsty for blood. He had become the 'Black Knight of Hungary', a famous and notable soldier in the Ottoman–Hungarian Wars. Ferenc helped conquer castles, lead armies, command sieges, and keep the Turks out of Hungary. Ferenc was now stationed at Castle Sarvar, on the Danube

River, by order of Emperor Rudolph II. Rudolph firmly believed he could unite all of Christendom against the Turks. However, he paid little attention to military strategy and became more reclusive, obsessed, and dedicated to expanding his art and science collection in the Royal Palace of Prague. Because of Rudolph's distractions, the Turkish war carried on for seven years, at a mighty cost.

In 1599, after 25 years, Elizabeth was the sole keeper of Castle Cachtice. With her husband away at war, she was in charge of all affairs, including hiring help, ensuring healthy crops, buying and selling goods, general security, and feeding the people within her walls and the surrounding villages.

"Did you want me to read the letter, my Lady?" Illona asked.

"No, give it here," Elizabeth said.

Illona handed Elizabeth the letter with a red wax seal. She smelled the letter and closed her eyes for a moment.

"Ah, yes, that is the smell of my war-wrought husband," Elizabeth said cheekily.

Illona could only smile at Elizabeth's comment.

"It smells of bloodshed and death," Elizabeth said with a smile. "I'm certain there will be tales of exotic lands, gruesome deaths, and heroic victories." Elizabeth opened the letter with a dagger-shaped letter opener.

"Hopefully, he has another tale like that of the Turks drowning in the River Kulpa," Illona said.

A few months prior, Elizabeth received a letter from Ferenc describing the incident at the River Kulpa. As Ferenc, the Black Knight of Hungary, retreated across the River Kulpa, the Sultan, Mehmed III, and his Ottoman forces gave chase. As the Turks began their gradual crossing, a terrible tempest caused a massive flood, killing thousands of crossing Turks. It looked like providence to the Hungarian people, who viewed Ferenc as a soldier touched by the Almighty.

"Let us be so lucky that an event like that ever happens again," Elizabeth said.

"God is with us, my Lady. The Ottoman Empire is weakening thanks to your devoted husband and Black Knight of Hungary," Illona said.

Elizabeth snickered at the comment. "A clever and brave soldier he is. To be a husband, he has yet to learn," she said, unfolding the letter with a smile.

> *My Dear Elizabeth,*
> *I am writing you this letter, not with a sad heart, but with great joy. Our armies continue to be victorious. The Turkish casualties continue to rise as we push on through this putrid hell. Emperor Rudolph II told me that Castle Sarvar was a significant target for our enemy, so he asked me to remain here and defend it for the foreseeable future. The good King has given me the title of "High Stable Master"; in return, the King wishes me to remain at Castle Sarvar and defend it with what he calls my "renowned skill and recognized reputation". I hope to return home within the year, but as you well know, I am of ample importance to the success and conquest of our Hungarian army. I hope you are well, and the children thrive with tutelage and gracefulness. I dearly miss our time together and the special entertainment we have shared. In the near future, I hope we can be reunited and*

celebrate with great feasts, entertainments, and festivities.
Sincerely and most devotedly your husband,
Ferenc

"My Ferenc must remain at Castle Sarvar," Elizabeth said to Illona.

"Why so, your Grace?"

"The King ordered him to stay because of his skills and reputation," Elizabeth said as she carelessly threw the letter on her desk. "The King values his leadership."

"Dinner will be served shortly, my Lady. Perhaps a hearty meal will change your disposition," Illona said delicately.

Elizabeth could only stare south out the window toward Castle Sarvar. She knew he was out there. She missed Ferenc's guidance and wisdom, but knew his legs were causing him significant pain. She wanted the war to end. She wanted to be able to take care of him.

"Your Grace?"

"Yes, Illona, dinner, of course. I shall be down momentarily," Elizabeth said.

"Yes, your Grace," Illona said as she exited the room.

Elizabeth stood motionless before the desk, her eyes fixed on her husband's letter. The ink had long dried, but the words were still fresh. A quiet ache began to swell in her chest; a deep, aching loneliness that pressed against her ribs and settled into her bones.

She reached out and lightly touched the edge of the paper, as if feeling it might somehow bring her closer to him. She missed him dearly. Not just his presence, but his warmth and his embrace always made the world feel less sharp and uncertain. She longed for how his calloused hands traced slow, familiar patterns along her skin, grounding her with each touch. The way his fingers tangled gently in her hair, and the way he brushed it back from her face made Elizabeth feel like the only person in the world who mattered. Now, there was only silence. A cold, lonely room and a letter lying on the old oak desk, like a ghost of the life they once shared.

—William Mowat—

Chapter 3 - The Britaine's New Man

Captain La Roche stood watch on the deck of the pirate vessel called the 'Britaine'. The bearded La Roche never took his eyes off the brilliant blue Mediterranean Sea. Emperor Rudolph II and his royal court had hired La Roche indirectly to inflict as much damage to the Ottoman Empire as possible.

The bright-eyed Captain peered through his looking glass while he stood proudly at the bow of his 60-gun ship. His duty was to search and destroy all Muslim vessels on the Mediterranean, especially those that carried precious cargo, including spice, liquor, jewels, weapons, fabric, or any other type of building material. He carefully and methodically patrolled the north coast of Africa, also known as the Barbary Coast. The Britaine was en route to Alexandria, in the heart of Egypt.

The Barbary Coast was a hostile place in 1599, full of local rulers, corsairs, pirates, and Islamic slave-traders looking to enslave Christian Europeans as a part of the Jihad holy war. European ships, especially those from Spain, France, Italy, and England, were frequent targets for Turkish pirates. Captain La Roche knew he and his crew would likely never see Europe or home again if captured.

"John Smith!" La Roche yelled towards the stern of the ship. "On deck!"

From the bowels of the ship, a young Englishman appeared on deck. Around 20 years old, he wore loose-fitting breeches, a ripped long-sleeved cotton shirt, and was buttoning his doublet as he approached the Captain.

"Aye, Captain. What's your command?" John responded.

"Fortune has thrown you in my way, and you have proved worthy in your short stay aboard our ship," said the Captain. "I am bound for Alexandria, and thereafter you may seek some profitable adventure. Or, in the coming months, I could drop you in Venice or somewhere in Italy, with a fat purse, should you agree to help us with our destiny and duty on the Barbary Coast. What say you?" the jolly La Roche asked.

The young man felt confident in his abilities, and the last few years had taught him a thing or two about sailing and combat. He felt fate and fortune had brought him aboard the Britaine, and he was now determined to support the cause of the Captain and his ship. "Captain La Roche, if you can get me to Italian shores with money in my pockets, I promise to serve you and protect this mighty Britaine in whatever type of engagement we find ourselves in."

"Alexandria is a week away. You will need to train with our cannons and crews," La Roche said. "Let's get everyone on deck and ready for some training," La Roche said.

During the next few days, John trained on the 60 guns of the Britaine. He got to know the crews, their mannerisms, and the routines that would secure their ability to win battles. John trained the other pirates in sword fighting and hand-to-hand combat. Though much younger than the crew, he was undoubtedly the most skilled and athletic. He also learned plenty of seamanship, including rigging the sails, controlling and reading the winds, watching the tell-tales, and helming the ship.

The Britaine sailed along the Straits of Otranto, off the coast of Italy, and Captain La Roche kept a close eye on the horizon, looking for a ship to prey upon. Hours passed; however, the seasoned captain did not lose his patience. He stood firm and poised at the bow of the Britaine. La Roche knew it would only be a matter of time.

La Roche pointed at the horizon. "There!" he yelled. "It looks Venetian!"

The Venetians had recently entered into a treaty with the Turks despite considerations and their own self-interest.

"It's one of those large Venetian cargo ships. Twice the size of our Britaine. But we have two big advantages," La Roche said.

"What's that?" one of La Roche's pirates asked.

"Speed and maneuverability," La Roche answered. "All pirates on deck!" he yelled.

All of Britaine's pirates, including the young, eager John, came on deck and were exposed to their oncoming prey.

"Remember why England beat Spain in the Atlantic Ocean? Speed and their ability to outmaneuver their enemy," La Roche said, pointing. "We will run alongside her and give the Venetian prey a nice couple of broadsides. Then, we'll throw our grappling hooks and begin the takeover."

"A bold plan, Captain," John said. "Come, men, let's prepare!"

John went below deck and organized the gun crews. They were a ragtag bunch of lowly sailors. Most were missing teeth, out of shape, and scruffy-looking, but they had trained for this moment. They had faith in John, their captain, and each other.

La Roche spent the next few minutes setting course for the takeover. Through deft command of his vessel, the Captain brought the Britaine into position alongside the Venetian ship, with its name *Argosy* inscribed upon the bow.

"Here she comes!" La Roche yelled. "Ready! Fire!"

John and the other pirates below fired their starboard guns and ran across the Venetian ship. The guns raked her from stern to bow. Wooden splinters flew everywhere, and the entire space between the ships billowed with smoke.

The Argosy's main mast fell as the rigging tangled itself with the cleats and hooks on deck. Venetian sailors were panicking all across the ship's deck, and it seemed like a perfect time to board the Argosy.

La Roche brought his vessel close alongside the Argosy and made fast with the grappling irons. The Argosy's crew, larger than the Britaine's, assembled on deck, ready to repel the French La Roche and his crew.

Gun smoke poured across both ships, and John carefully calculated his next move. "Prepare the grappling hooks!" he shouted.

"Lead them, my boy!" La Roche cried. "Don't give them an inch!"

"Loose!" John yelled as a dozen pirates wound up and launched their grappling hooks. Almost all the lines were successful in taking hold. Once the men had the hooks set, it was nearly impossible for the Venetians to move them. The two ships drew closer as the pirates began tying off the ropes.

The entire crew of the Britaine drew swords and charged onto the Venetian deck with their best battle cries. The battle began with the first wave of pirates being repelled by the

Venetians. John and Captain La Roche led the second wave with more eager pirates. There was furious hand-to-hand combat on the deck. The clashing of swords and musket-fire erupted, as the bodies began to fall.

Captain La Roche and John, by his side, shoulder-to-shoulder, fought their way towards the deck where the commander of the Argosy stood.

"We're about to be cut off from our men!" La Roche yelled.

"We need to break through to the other side!" John yelled to La Roche.

"Men! On me!" La Roche yelled. "Charge!"

The pirates pushed the Argosy seamen back with a fierce charge. Clanging of swords and the smoke from small firearms filled the deck, causing mass confusion amongst the sailors. The pirates began pushing the Venetian crew off the deck into the salty, turbulent sea below.

Captain La Roche pushed back to the deck of the Britaine and ordered his guns reloaded. The Britaine gave way and poured two broadsides into the injured Argosy. The Venetian ship began to sink.

Many of the Venetian crew were dead, injured, or starting to throw their hands in the air. Once more, a few more pirates threw grappling irons and pulled the Argosy directly alongside the Britaine.

After nearly an hour of fierce fighting, the Venetian crew finally surrendered, and the Captain of the Argosy gave up his sword. Twenty Venetians lay dead, many more were severely injured, and the rest were desperately trying to plug the holes in the hull of the sinking ship.

Captain La Roche had lost fifteen of his crew, and eight had sword wounds, but it was a significant victory for the

French Captain. He secured the prisoners, tended the wounded and began off-loading the Argosy cargo onto his ship. They discovered crates of silk, velvets, and other rich fabrics. There were hundreds of jewels, works of art, and a considerable quantity of gold and silver.

"Well done today, my friends. Extra rations of wine for everyone!" La Roche yelled.

"Hooray!" the pirate crew shouted.

"John, your nation, the Holy Roman Empire, and Jesus Christ himself would be proud of what you have done today," La Roche said, putting his hand on John's shoulder.

After nearly 24 gruelling hours, Captain La Roche finally gave the order to cut the Argosy loose, letting her drift on the open sea with her battered crew still aboard. Once proud and sea-worthy, the vessel was now listing heavily to one side, her sails torn to ribbons and her timbers scorched and splintered from the fight. La Roche had considered towing her into port as a formal prize, but the damage was too extensive.

The young, proud John Smith watched from the deck of the Britaine as the Argosy receded into the misty horizon, her silhouette a broken shadow against the rising sun.

Despite the loss of the prize ship itself, the raid had not been without reward. John's personal share of the spoils came to 500 gold pieces. He was also gifted a small, iron-clasped box glinting with jewels given to him by La Roche. True to his word, La Roche had seen that the young Englishman was well compensated for his bravery and resolve during the battle. La Roche had taken a liking to John and was impressed by his steadiness in the chaos of combat and his loyalty to the crew of the Britaine.

As they approached the Italian coast days later, La Roche turned to him and said, "You've earned your purse, John

Smith. More than earned it. You came aboard a boy. Now you walk ashore a man, with gold in your pocket and salt in your blood."

–William Mowat–

Chapter 4 - Beware the Ides of March

Peter Dowling and his daughter Margaret stood shoulder to shoulder amidst the crowd of Londoners, their eyes fixed on the unfolding drama atop the new wooden stage of the Globe. The midsummer sun filtered through the open roof above, casting golden light onto the actors and lending a natural brilliance to the scene that seemed almost divine.

Onstage, the world of ancient Rome had come to life with astonishing vigour. Brutus and the other conspirators, draped in flowing togas of cream and crimson, circled the fallen figure of Caesar. Their garments, though stylized for the English audience, evoked the grandeur of a lost empire; draped folds of cloth pinned with golden brooches, leather sandals laced up to the calf, and wide leather belts slung across their chests.

The actor playing Caesar lay motionless, his tunic stained with theatrical blood that glistened under the afternoon light. Gasps had rippled through the crowd at the moment of betrayal, when Brutus stepped forward with a trembling hand and joined the others in their terrible pact. "Et tu, Brute?" had fallen like a thunderclap.

Now, Marc Antony stood above the slain leader, his expression caught somewhere between grief and fury. The actor wore a soldier's tunic dyed in the Roman red, a golden sash across his chest, and leather armour, completed with stylized eagle motifs. His posture was commanding, his voice powerful, reverberating against the timbered walls of the Globe as he raised his arms to address the crowd:

> *Friends, Romans, countrymen, lend me your ears;*
> *I come to bury Caesar, not to praise him.*
> *The evil that men do lives after them;*
> *The good is oft interred with their bones;*
> *So let it be with Caesar. The noble Brutus*
> *Hath told you Caesar was ambitious:*
> *If it were so, it was a grievous fault,*
> *And grievously hath Caesar answer'd it.*

Peter turned and admired his daughter, looking at the performance. "Watch how he uses emotion to appeal to the people."

Margaret stared in awe at the actor portraying Marc Antony as he peered down at Caesar's body. She imagined herself on stage and how exhilarating it might be, though acting would be nearly impossible for her, considering men portrayed all the female roles.

> *Here, under leave of Brutus and the rest—*
> *For Brutus is an honourable man;*
> *So are they all, all honourable men—*
> *Come I to speak in Caesar's funeral.*
> *He was my friend, faithful and just to me:*
> *But Brutus says he was ambitious;*
> *And Brutus is an honourable man.*
> *He hath brought many captives home to Rome*

Whose ransoms did the general coffers fill:
Did this in Caesar seem ambitious?

"See how Anthony uses repetition to persuade the crowd?" Peter whispered again.

Standing and sitting, the crowd watched the powerful, charismatic actor deliver his funeral speech in perfect tempo and rhythm.

When that the poor have cried, Caesar hath wept:
Ambition should be made of sterner stuff:
Yet Brutus says he was ambitious;
And Brutus is an honourable man.
You all did see that on the Lupercal
I thrice presented him a kingly crown,
Which he did thrice refuse: was this ambition?
Yet Brutus says he was ambitious;
And, sure, he is an honourable man.
I speak not to disprove what Brutus spoke,
But here I am to speak what I do know.
You all did love him once, not without cause:
What cause withholds you then, to mourn for him?
O judgment! thou art fled to brutish beasts,
And men have lost their reason. Bear with me;
My heart is in the coffin there with Caesar,
And I must pause till it comes back to me."

"You see how he uses the crowd's emotions and pathos to turn them against Brutus. Brilliant!" Peter said to his daughter.

"Shhhhh!" Margaret snapped.

Peter smiled at his daughter's interest in the historical play and turned his attention back to the stage.

The performance surged toward its climactic conclusion. The tension of civil war unravelled across the stage in a whirlwind of swords, betrayal, and impassioned speeches. With the final line echoing into the stillness, the audience stood in stunned silence for a heartbeat before a roaring wave of applause surged from every corner of the Globe.

The whole ensemble returned to the stage, breathless and beaming, their sweat-slicked costumes catching the golden light. Each actor bowed deeply, some in pairs and some clutching war props. As the actor who had embodied Julius Caesar stepped forward for his final bow, draped in regal crimson and gold, his face still streaked with stage blood. The audience, again, roared with delight.

Then, a new figure emerged from the backstage area's shadows. He wore a fine black doublet with decorative stitching, knee-length breeches of deep burgundy, and a stiff, starched white collar that framed his smiling face. His pointed leather shoes clicked softly against the boards as he crossed the stage, and his dark eyes gleamed with quiet mischief. A few murmurs rustled through the crowd, curious at this late arrival.

He moved with the casual confidence of someone entirely at home before an audience. With a warm smile, he waved to each theatre deck: the pit, the middle gallery, and the lofty top tier. He bowed to the left, then to the right, turned full centre. Slowly, with deliberate theatricality, he stroked his chin whiskers and pulled a large eagle-feather quill from behind his back.

The moment crystallized. A collective realization swept over the audience like a ripple across water.

Margaret clutched her father's arm. "Father," she whispered, "that's him! That's Shakespeare!"

A ripple of gasps, cheers, and spontaneous applause broke across the audience like thunder. William Shakespeare, playwright, poet, provocateur, had stepped out from the wings of his own creation. The man who had given them Caesar's fall, Brutus' torment, and Antony's fury stood in the flesh, bowing humbly before the people he had moved to laughter, tears, and reflection.

Margaret's eyes shone. "He's real," she whispered, scarcely believing it.

"Friends, countrymen!" Shakespeare yelled. "You have lent me your ears, you have journeyed with Caesar, now I have come to humbly thank you, beautiful Londoners. Without you, none of this would ever be possible."

Shakespeare gave one final bow, hand over heart, before vanishing again into the shadows, leaving behind the echo of his art and the magic of a well-told story.

Margaret turned to her father and smiled with tears of joy streaming down her face.

—William Mowat—

Chapter 5 - The Holy Roman Empire

The Habsburgs had ruled the Holy Roman Empire for hundreds of years. Rudolph II, a member of the Habsburg dynasty, ruled from his court in Prague, a complex place in the late 16th century. It was filled with intellectuals, artists, politicians, royal patrons, and nobles. The Holy Roman Emperor, Rudolf II, blended his love of art and science with political and religious tensions around the kingdom.

Rudolf was eccentric, introverted, sensitive, and an isolated ruler who loved to collect art, antiquities, and animals from around the world. His collection was unique and varied, containing thousands of books, art pieces, and scientific instruments. Tigers and lions roamed the grounds, peacocks strutted through gardens, and all types of amphibians and reptiles swam freely in nearby ponds.

The Roman Emperor also welcomed the world's most intelligent thinkers: alchemists, philosophers, magicians, and astronomers, including the newly arrived Tycho Brahe, a Danish astronomer known for his accuracy and comprehension of astronomical calculations. Rudolph II obsessively wanted to unlock the mysteries of the universe.

Rudolph also had syphilis and was, oftentimes, both manic and reclusive in his decision-making. Generations of royal inbreeding had led to several abnormalities within the various European kingdoms, including the Habsburgs. His introverted nature and hyperintelligence led to indecision, poor health, anxiety, and bouts of paranoia.

The conflict that was once a brief campaign had now escalated into the Long Turkish War. Despite his limited understanding of the military terrain and the strategic complexities involved, Emperor Rudolph II remained resolute in his desire to defend Christendom against the advancing forces of the Ottoman Empire. His determination, however, was not matched by effective leadership or decisive action. Although a more committed and strategically engaged ruler might have brought the war to a swifter conclusion, Rudolph allowed personal interests and courtly distractions to overshadow the demands of warfare.

The Prague Court on this day would host a series of military leaders to conference and discuss the ongoing conflict with the Turks, whom they had been battling for eight years. Rudolph II was convinced he could defeat the Turks and bring a new crusade to the east. His brother, Archduke Matthias, was concerned about Rudolph's deteriorating health and his management of the Kingdom. He had travelled to Prague with Ferenc Nadasdy, Elizabeth Bathory's husband, to discuss tactics in the upcoming months.

Ferenc Nadasdy and his riders galloped proudly on the cobblestone streets with a dozen of his best riders, waving the Order of the Dragon flag and the banners of Hungary and Transylvania. Ferenc had long, straight black hair and a beard, giving him a dark, mysterious, imposing appearance. Given Ferenc's importance in fighting the Turks and his family's influence, Rudolph II formally welcomed the various leaders.

Horns sounded and soldiers stood in procession as Ferenc and others entered the royal courtyard. Horses aligned side-by-side, and the soldiers saluted their Holy Roman Emperor. Ferenc, dressed in rich military and noble attire, felt a surge of confidence from the horns and the welcoming. He dismounted his horse and approached Rudolph II and his brother, Matthias, at the top of the palace steps.

"The Holy Roman Empire, the King of Bohemia, Hungary, and Croatia; Margrave of Moravia; and the Archduke of Austria welcomes you to his royal court," the Royal Herald cried.

Ferenc bowed before the King.

"My Lord, Count Nadasdy, Palatine of Hungary, and Royal Advisor of Military Affairs," the Herald announced.

Rudolph and Matthias bowed their heads at the newly arrived Nadasdy. Both brothers were strikingly similar in appearance, with protruding underbites, round bellies, and red beards, but couldn't be more different in temperament, decisiveness, and overall leadership.

The Habsburgs, Europe's most powerful and influential royal family, had kings or queens in nearly every European country. All of them understood that Ferenc Nadasdy was of vital military importance. His loyal defence of Hungary was on the frontier lands between Christendom and the Muslim world. All of the Habsburgs valued Ferenc's qualities and ability to win battles. Nadasdy also provided the royal Habsburgs with abundant taxes and plundered gold and silver from the Ottoman Empire. Ferenc was funding a strapped Holy Royal Empire, so they left him alone to continue his ways, whatever they may be.

The ceremony continued as the powerful men entered the Royal Court, where they viewed palace halls filled with a vast collection of priceless art, intricate machines, gems, and taxidermy. Yet, the wonders from around the world were marvelled at by very few, since access was restricted to royal patrons, the curators, and the Emperor himself.

Ferenc admired the paintings of Leonardo da Vinci and Hans von Aachen. The convoy passed massive statues of Zeus and Athena from ancient Greece and royal sarcophagi from Egypt. They passed through a room full of astronomical instruments, perpetual motion machines, and various alchemy tools and experiments. It was too much for Ferenc to absorb. Though a thousand questions spun through his head, he knew best to keep quiet and let the royal brothers do most of the talking.

The next room was fascinating for Ferenc. A massive room full of dozens of fossils, taxidermy from around the world, and artificial wonders from strange, mystical places. On display were unicorn horns, which were actually taken from narwhal whales a century earlier, and a dragon skull, the fossil of an extinct dinosaur. Ferenc paused at the massive skull and pondered his family lineage and the story of St. George, which made the biblical narrative much more real. "Incredible," he said to himself.

Ferenc continued through the room and paused in awe of the exotic birds Rudolph had imported from the jungles of Southeast Asia.

As they slowly walked from room to room, saying very little, Ferenc observed Rudolph's introverted, compulsive behaviour towards his collection. Rudolph would slightly alter the position of objects; he would run his fingers along items, checking for dust, and stick his face within inches of some items for extreme close-ups.

Eventually, the dozen leaders made it to the grand hall with a central marble-slab table with a diverse spread of cheeses, fruits, nuts, and meats. The men all sat down once Rudolph had taken his position at the head of the grand table.

"Welcome to Prague, gentlemen. I'm glad you've arrived safe and sound," Rudolph said. "And you've enjoyed my collection of wonders."

"We thank your majesty for such a grand tour through the marvellous collection," Ferenc said.

"We are experimenting day and night, and we believe we have found the alchemy to turn iron to gold," Rudolph said. "We are ever so close to discovering the Philosopher's Stone, I just know it."

"I see, your Grace," Ferenc said with a nod.

"My brother has hired Europe's greatest fools. They fill his ears with lies, just to please his Majesty. I would have the criminals killed," Matthias said, sneering towards his brother.

"I've hired the best scientists and mathematicians from around the Empire," Rudolph said proudly. "We are on the verge of many great discoveries."

"My brother has almost entirely forgotten about our war with the Turks," Matthias said with a smirk.

"I have not forgotten about dear Hungary," Rudolph said with assurance in the direction of Ferenc. "I have hired 10,000 new mercenaries from England, France, Spain, and Sweden. I intend to flush the Muslims right out of Europe and back to where they came from."

"10,000 troops would do us well on the Danube River, my Lord. Castle Sarvar is a stronghold that desperately needs reinforcements," Ferenc responded. "All our young men have enlisted; the only people that remain in our villages are the old and young girls."

"I shall guide these mercenaries to Hungary upon their arrival," Matthias said, reassuring Ferenc. "The Earl of Meldritch and you shall lead them to victory. I am certain."

The Emperor, Matthias, Nadasdy, and the other lords of the Empire discussed timelines, money, taxes, and the recent plague that had broken out in Prague. As they discussed the devastating nature of the sickness, one of Rudolph's doctors came barging into the room carrying a vial of something indistinguishable.

"My Lord, my King, I've done it!" the doctor said, holding the vial in the air. "A perfect medicine for bodies that are sick. All the infirmaries and sanitoriums are to be relieved!"

"Good doctor, what is in this elixir?" Rudolph asked.

"Cinnamon, ginger root, elder root, and calamus dissolved in a decoction of lemon juice and strong wine," the doctor said with a smile.

"Has it worked on everyone?" Rudolph questioned.

"Only those who take a half-pint before meals during the moon in Cancer, Leo or Virgo," the doctor said, still smiling.

Matthias looked at Ferenc and frowned at the thought of an elixir only working during the moon when certain stars were in the sky. "You see who my brother invites here."

Chapter 6 - The Scarlet Secret

Elizabeth Bathory had learned her husband, Ferenc Nadasdy, had travelled to Prague to meet with Rudolph to coordinate the campaign against the Ottoman Empire. It was no surprise to Elizabeth, as Ferenc had been gone most of the last decade.

Their children had grown, except for Paul, their youngest. He was still so young; he had only met his father a handful of times. The other Bathory children were treated more like pawns in a giant chess match than children. As with Elizabeth and Ferenc's arranged marriage, family prominence and preservation of titles was of the utmost importance. Their firstborn had been married to Nikola VI Zrinski, a Croatian Count. Both Anna and Katalin were being raised and tutored as high nobility in Prague, apart from their family. Elizabeth did not have time to be a devoted mother; she shouldered too much responsibility in the Kingdom of Hungary.

Elizabeth was writing a letter to a far-off Imre Megyery, one of her estate's most trusted employees. She entrusted him to buy and sell beef, wheat, and anything else that needed clever planning and proper business tactics. Imre was intelligent, diplomatic, and had incredible business sense. He was a highly valued employee to Elizabeth and Ferenc.

Frustrated, she crumpled up the letter she was writing and pitched it across the room. She rose from the desk, looked through her bookshelf, and pulled a large, leather-bound book. She sat down and began to read. After only a few minutes, she lost interest and tossed the book aside.

Her mind was clearly racing and unfocused. She once again stood up and paced her study. She moved to the window and looked way into the distance at the Village of Cachtice and gave a little smile. She gazed into a small mirror that hung from the wall near the window and began analyzing the contours and lines on her face.

Elizabeth stared intensely at herself. She stretched her skin off her cheeks and pulled her eyelids back. The intense analysis of her face did not make the Countess happy or comfortable with her appearance. She convinced herself she was no longer young.

"Dorka!" Elizabeth yelled.

A moment later, Dorka entered Elizabeth's study. Dorka was another of Elizabeth's oldest and most trusted servants. She wore a long black dress and a headscarf that most of her other servants wore. Most peasants and servants were terrified of Dorka, as she had Elizabeth's ear and was as mean as the devil himself.

"How may I be of service, your highness?" Dorka asked in her deep, raspy voice.

"Dorka, bring the girl that Fitzko found me last week," Elizabeth said, still looking at herself in the mirror.

"Right away, your highness," Dorka said.

Dorka left the room and went down the cold steps of the castle stairwell. She moved with excited anticipation through the rooms of the lower level and eventually through the kitchen and pantry, past the storage closets, and finally came to an unsuspecting stairwell. The dark steps led down to a dimly lit stone hallway with dirt floors and a few solid oak doors, all locked and chained.

It was much colder in the dark depths of the mountain castle, as Dorka made her way to the last door at the end of the hallway guarded by a giant, bearded man. He saw Dorka coming and straightened his posture. Benedek had been a servant since he was a little boy and did whatever he was told, without question.

"You're not sleeping, are you, Benedek?" Dorka snapped.

"No, my Lady," he said, sticking his chin in the air.

"Open the door," Dorka demanded.

"Yes, my Lady." Benedek turned around and opened the door with the key that hung around his neck. The door led to a small hallway with a series of smaller doors. Dorka entered and peered through one of the small, barred windows. She removed the deadbolt and opened the door to a filthy, young girl wearing the clothes of a country peasant. Her head drooped down with her hands shackled in irons hanging from the brick wall. At first, it appeared she might be dead.

Dorka unlocked the heavy cuffs, and the girl fell to the floor with a slap.

"Get up, darling. You're coming with me," Dorka said, picking the girl up around the shoulder. "It must be your lucky day."

"Please, let me go," the weakened girl quietly said as she mustered the strength and rose to her feet. Blood oozed from her face, and there was a series of gashes on her neck and wrists.

Dorka and the girl moved back through the cell and past Benedek.

"No one in or out without my permission or Lady Bathory's. Is that understood, Benedek?" Dorka coldly demanded.

"Yes, Ladyship," he receded.

"Good, do not disappoint me," Dorka said as she walked back up through the castle with the frail girl.

Benedek stood upright as straight as he could.

A few minutes later, Dorka and the girl came through the study doors to Elizabeth, who stood gazing out her window. The girl was terrified, barefoot and shivering, but seemed to be getting her bearings.

Elizabeth turned and stared at the frightened girl. "No need to be afraid," the Countess reassuringly said.

The shivering girl dropped her gaze to the stone floor, hoping to avoid confrontation with the Countess.

"You smell like feces, my dear," Elizabeth heartlessly said. "We shall have to get you into a bath."

The girl began to whimper, sensing the cold nature of Bathory.

"No need to be shy, dear. How are you?" Elizabeth asked again.

Finally, the young, afraid girl spoke: "I am here to serve. I will do anything you ask of me, your Grace. I talk about nothing but the good word of God and respect you most devotedly, your Highness. I have come here to learn and become a lady under your tutelage. Please let it be known if there is anything I might do."

"Dorka, bring my hairbrush from my vanity at once," the Countess demanded.

"Right away," Dorka said, leaving the room.

Elizabeth sat at her desk and waited until Dorka returned. "I was initially unsure of you, my dear, but you have convinced me otherwise. Come here, my dear, do not be afraid."

The pale, peasant girl approached Elizabeth slowly as Dorka arrived with a hairbrush.

"Have you ever brushed a noble woman's hair before?" Elizabeth asked with a smile.

"No, my lady," the girl said shyly.

"How does my hair look?" Elizabeth asked.

"Most splendid, your Grace," the girl responded.

"You may begin," Elizabeth said.

The girl slowly and timidly began to brush the Countess's long black hair with strokes across the back of her head, while Dorka watched from the doorway.

Elizabeth closed her eyes as she enjoyed the first few relaxing strokes. "You are a charming young lady. Ferenc would love you. My absentee husband has just sent word that he will not be returning anytime soon and will likely miss another Christmas here at home," Elizabeth explained.

"I'm sorry to hear that, my Lady," the girl said, still brushing Elizabeth's hair.

"Ferenc is an even bigger monster than I am. He loves torturing his captured enemies. He says it 'brings him a sense of calm'. After his numerous battles, removing the heads of savages, slashing at the bowels of enemies, and pushing our foes out of Hungary, it all must leave him on tremendous highs. I suppose he needs to come down somehow." There was a pause as the girl continued to brush. "He says the entertainments dull the senses of battle and brings his nerves down afterwards. And who am I to argue?"

There was a prolonged period when the two did not say anything to each other. The peasant girl continued to brush nervously as Elizabeth enjoyed the sensation of the bristles moving along her skull.

"Your hair does not require my brushing, my Lady. It is quite lovely as it is," she said, trying to sway the Countess to favour.

"Thank you, my dear," Elizabeth said coldly.

The young, afraid girl was extremely cautious with each stroke. Suddenly and unknowingly, the brush got caught in a knot of hair and snapped the Countess's head back.

Before the girl could apologize, Elizabeth rose, spun around, and faced the young girl.

The young girl froze, at a complete loss for words. After a brief, yet lasting pause, Elizabeth struck the peasant across the face; blood from her nose splashed onto the floor and all over the exposed pale arm of Elizabeth.

"Clumsy little harlot. You shall pay dearly for this insult!" the irate Elizabeth screamed.

"I'm sorry, your Grace," the crying girl said.

"Dorka, take this filth to her chamber and chain her to the cold, damp walls and slit her throat," Elizabeth demanded. "Send Fitzko and Illona to my study at once," she added.

Dorka grabbed the arm of the frightened, bloody girl and pulled her out of Elizabeth's study.

Elizabeth was fuming until she observed the blood splattered on her arm. She initially wiped the blood off, but then smeared it in circular patterns. Squinting at the area, a look of enlightenment came over her face. She tilted her head to get a different vantage point and seemed impressed by the perspective. Feeling a little joy, Elizabeth sat down at her desk.

Fitzko, a four-foot, deformed dwarf, entered Elizabeth's study. His face was gnarled, his cleft-lip prominent, and he walked with a gimp. Helena, another black-dressed, older servant to the Countess, followed him.

"Hello, my Lady," Helena said.

Elizabeth turned her head to the newly arrived servants. "Helena, Fitzko, come look at this," Elizabeth said.

Fitzko and Helena approached Elizabeth, who was staring at her arm. They both looked on in puzzlement.

"What are we observing?" Fitzko asked.

"My arm, its complexion. Do you see it?" Elizabeth asked. "Blood from that wretched peasant girl. It has made my skin appear younger. Do you see it?"

Fitzko and Helena looked at one another.

"The Great Book of Shadows describes the restorative nature of a virgin's blood. The Goddess Hecate bathed in the blood of virgins," Helena said. "Perhaps..."

"Yes, my Lady. Your one arm appears younger and more vibrant than the other," Fitzko added.

"Remarkable," Elizabeth said, fixated on her arm.

Later that evening, several servants carried a sealed wooden casket into the courtyard of Castle Cachtice and set it down.

On assignment to lead a funeral procession at the castle, Pastor Istivan, the local village priest of Cachtice, noticed the commotion and hurried to see the new coffin and the recently deceased.

"My goodness, what has happened? Who might this person be? Another dead?" the pastor inquired. "Should we not have an open casket to give the proper eulogy?"

Just then, Elizabeth came through the castle doors, took him by the arm, and walked him into the courtyard.

"Dear Pastor, Your Holiness, this young person had a severe case of cholera. We closed the casket so as not to alarm anyone in the castle. You know what panic can do amongst the people," Elizabeth cleverly said.

"I understand, your Highness. It seems Cholera has gripped the entire world, especially here at Castle Cachtice," Pastor Istivan replied.

"There have been many deaths, Pastor Istivan; too many to count. If you could lead our procession and give the girl the proper burial she needs, it would mean the world," Elizabeth said.

"Of course, your Grace. I shall lead the procession and sing our traditional funeral hymns," Pastor Istivan answered, as he spun around and made his way to the newly arrived coffin.

Chapter 7 - Whispers to a Wild Heart

John Smith found himself wealthy for the first time in his life. He already had an adventurous spirit, but now he had the means to fund his ambitions. John Smith had cordially said goodbye to Captain La Roche and the crew of the Britaine and set off on his own.

After his father passed away, John Smith took to the seas when he was just 16. He served in the army of Henry IV of France against the Spanish. He trained on horses, mastered jousting and sword fighting, and recently plundered ships on the Mediterranean. Now, driven to support the Holy Roman Empire against the Ottoman Empire and desperate for action, he took his newly earned 500 gold pieces and set out for the Royal Court of the Habsburgs to seek work as a mercenary.

It was a two-week journey from the shores of the Mediterranean to the Royal Court of Prague. He enjoyed being on his feet, walking from village to village, learning new customs and foreign languages. He was trying new exotic foods and sleeping in the finest inns. He was sleeping soundly and was happier than he had ever been.

Smith finally arrived in the beautiful city of Prague and checked into an inn for a few nights. He took to the rich streets, admired the architecture, and looked forward to a big, hearty meal. The next day, he would meet with military advisors at the Royal Court of Rudolph II and likely be assigned duty within the week. Smith was excited to join the army once again. He was eager to suit up and engage in battle, draw his sword, and clash with the enemy. His sense of adventure was at an all-time high.

As he waited for his orders, he explored the lavish streets of Prague. The city piqued his interest with extravagant shops, bakeries, taverns, and various businesses. Smith strolled and came across a large mansion on the outskirts of town. A large crowd had gathered, and two men were trying to wrangle a youthful, energetic horse. They were obviously having difficulty holding the excited, bucking horse.

Smith admired the black, silky coat of the horse and understood the two men had not broken the animal. A handsomely dressed man, wearing a velvet robe and freshly polished leather boots, watched with disappointment from the porch. Assuming he was likely the Lord of the Manor, the ambitious John Smith approached the front step.

"What a magnificent animal, my Lord," John said.

"I have been swindled. This beast seems incapable of training," the finely dressed man said in response.

"My Lord, my name is John Smith, from England. If it pleases your lordship, I should like to try and break this animal."

"John Smith from England. You must be here to support our brethren of the Holy Roman Empire. Well, I am the Earl of Meldritch. This Barbary steed has the devil inside of him. I would not trust myself upon the back of such a beast for all the wealth of the Indies."

"With your lordship's consent, I would like to give it my best," replied John.

"Bring this man a saddle!" the Earl of Meldritch yelled.

John stepped through the corral fence. Knowing that building trust was the most critical factor when breaking a wild stallion, he started talking to the horse immediately, stroking its cheeks to communicate his peaceful intent. The horse began to kick wildly with its hind legs. "Now, I have you," John said in a soft tone. "You're in good hands now. I am your friend and I will not let anything happen to you. Trust me, and I will trust you."

The horse yielded to John's soft-spoken words. He put the saddle on the horse's back with some difficulty as he continued speaking softly.

"As soon as I get on the horse, let go," John said to the two men holding onto the reins.

John hopped on the saddle, and the two men let go. The animal lost composure and began to jump up and down, as John struggled to stay on. It started spinning wildly, trying to throw John from its back. It reared up on its hind legs, but John held on with all his might.

John's training in England was paying off. He held on tight and made it safely through all of the animal's antics. Eventually, John ordered the gate open, and he and the black beast flew out of sight.

The Earl of Meldritch couldn't believe his eyes. "Now that is a horseman!" he yelled. "I hope he comes back alive."

John rode the excited black stallion through the neighbouring meadows and the forested tree lines. Throughout the entire ride, he talked and encouraged the powerful horse. Together they meandered through orchards and streams. They crossed bridges and galloped along dirt roads. John began showing the horse the basic commands of turning, starting, and stopping. John felt the cool nip of the evening air, and the excitement made him smile.

After an hour of hard riding, Smith and the horse returned to the Prague mansion. The lord of the manor stepped onto the porch to see the returning rider coming down the pebbled laneway.

"The valiant rider returns!" the Earl yelled as he noticed the horse's tempered demeanour. "You've bonded with the beast!"

"He just needed to get out and get the feel," Smith responded. "Right, boy?" he said softly to the horse.

"Did you have any difficulty subduing the steed? Take any falls or tumbles?" the Earl asked.

"None at all. The horse is smart, trustworthy, and sure-footed," John replied. "They learn from our words, my Lord."

Smith rode the horse back and forth, parading for the Earl. He demonstrated the horse's ability to start and stop, go left or right, and be calm with a gentle touch.

"You see, my Lord. He is no beast at all!" Smith said.

The Earl shook his head in disbelief and smiled at the young stranger.

John dismounted and guided the horse back into the corral, where it immediately went for a drink of water.

"Unbelievable! You truly are a horseman," the Earl said, approaching the pen.

"Thank you, my Lord," John said. "I had masterful training in England and on the battlefield, alongside Henry IV of France, against the Spaniards."

"Remarkable. What brings you to Prague? I assume you are a mercenary soldier," the Earl inquired.

"I'm looking to join a contingency and fight the Turks, my Lord," John said. "Just waiting on orders."

"How would you like to join my cavalry regiment, he asked. "Your skills are well above average, and we need the best horsemen to fight against the skilled riders of the east."

"I would be honoured," John replied. The young soldier was elated at the opportunity.

"Excellent, John Smith. As a token of my loyalty, I present to you the black horse you've just broken," the Earl said. "He will be your companion and friend as you charge into many victories."

"Thank you, your Excellency," John smiled at the thought of being on top of such a magical horse and fighting with the cavalry against the Ottomans. "He is magnificent."

"John Smith, step inside and let us share a bottle of wine. Only the finest Burgundies."

"I would be honoured," Smith said as he brushed the dust from his jacket, stomped the mud off his boots, and walked inside with the Earl.

Smith was now attached to the Imperial army of the Holy Roman Empire, in an honourable capacity, and was thrilled at the prospects of his future and fighting the enemy.

—William Mowat—

Chapter 8 - Quickly's Charm

Peter Dowling and his daughter Margaret walked the muddy streets of London chatting about work, theatre, art, politics, and current affairs. They spoke about Sir Walter Raleigh's expeditions to the New World, Queen Elizabeth's deteriorating health, and who might be next in line for the crown of England. They never ran out of things to talk about.

Peter's correspondence with the Habsburgs in Prague resulted in the offer of a tutoring position with a prominent Hungarian family. Peter had yet to tell his daughter about the offer and their future adventure together. He was just waiting for the perfect time to break the news.

The father and daughter entered the Crown and Pheasant tavern, where they would frequently get a bowl of stew or dine on some salted fish or fried potatoes. Mistress Quickly ran the tavern with an iron fist. She did not tolerate abusive language, drunken or boorish behaviour, or people who didn't pay their tabs.

Quickly greeted Peter and Margaret with a beaming, rosy-cheeked smile. "Well, aren't you two a sight for sore eyes?" Quickly said.

"Hello, Miss Quickly. How is the stew tonight?" Peter asked.

"Well, I spent the whole night making pie shells, and we stuffed them with pork hearts, liver, potatoes, and onions. They're almost all gone, so you better have at her!" Quickly said with a wink.

"Sounds delightful, Miss Quickly," Peter said.

"So, what'll you have?" she asked.

"Two of those fine pies will be delightful," Peter said. "I will also have a pint of your finest ale."

"Sure thing," Quickly said as she left toward the kitchen.

The two sat down and smiled at the thought of a hearty meal to come.

"Margaret, I've got some wonderful news," Peter started.

"What is it?" Margaret excitedly asked.

"I've been offered a guaranteed teaching contract to tutor an elite family that pays ten times what I am making now."

"Well, that's terrific!" Margaret exclaimed. "Is it in Westminster, or Essex, Cornhill, or wait, is it the Covent Garden?"

"It's not in England, my dear. It is in Europe," Peter said.

"Paris! No, wait, Rome? Antwerp? Spain?"

"A royal family in Hungary!" Peter exclaimed.

"Hungary?" Margaret said with a frown.

"The Habsburgs. The Royal family of the Holy Roman Empire," Peter said.

Margaret still did not look impressed. "Why do the royals of the Roman Empire need a teacher like you?"

"Well, because I'm England's smartest man," Peter proudly joked.

"That's not funny," Margaret said.

"I have been hired to tutor a noble, young family to learn English, Latin, and Greek because they do not have time to raise their children while battling the hordes of Turkish forces. You are to be my official assistant and secretary. I will hire you, and you will earn a lavish income on your tutoring adventure. You can help organize my schedule, mark notes, and build lessons."

"What if I decline the position?" Margaret cheekily responded.

"Well, you would be certifiably insane, not to mention foolish, to decline such a rare opportunity. This whole experience will help fund your education and afford us a cottage in the countryside," Peter said. He had always dreamed of a quiet cottage, with old oak trees, and a lake to cast a line into.

Margaret sat and stared at the wooden table in front of her. Miss Quickly returned with two steaming meat pies and put them down in front of Peter and Margaret.

"What's gotten into little Margaret?" Quickly said, looking at Margaret staring at the table.

"She's just thinking," Peter said. "Maybe a little too hard."

"Father here wants us to go to Hungary to make a lavish wage tutoring noble children," Margaret told Miss Quickly.

"Beware of seeking fame and fortune in the belly of the beast," Quickly said with a wink. "A strange, foreign land, the Far East is, full of mystery and dark secrets."

"The mystery excites me," Peter replied.

"Excites you, maybe," Margaret said with a frown.

"Well, enjoy the pies," Quickly said, leaving the table. "Lighten up, darling."

Margaret turned her head up and looked at her father. "I guess I'm going to have to quit my job," she said, "I love my job."

"I'm sure it will be available when we return. I will talk with your employer. You just need to leave amicably. Tell them there is a temporary contract abroad with your father," Peter said. "They should understand."

"I don't want to leave London," Margaret said.

"Think of the adventure. We're going to sail halfway around the world. We'll take a horse and buggy through the Carpathian Mountains to a huge royal castle," Peter said.

"A castle?" Margaret's eyes lit up.

"A massive, elegant, decorated castle. With servants, lavish meals, and linens made of the finest silks," Peter answered. "You will be like a princess."

"A princess? I think I might be able to handle that for a while," Margaret said, taking a bite of her meat pie.

"I thought you'd come around," Peter said, taking a big bite of his.

"Will I have my own servants?" Margaret asked.

"Now, let's not get ahead of ourselves," Peter said with a smirk.

Chapter 9 - The Count's Return

Count Ferenc Nadasdy had returned home to Castle Cachtice, accompanied by the Earl of Meldritch, thousands of mercenaries, and John Smith on his new black stallion. It would be the last stop before their destination of Castle Sarvar, Nadasdy's station on the Danube River, on the frontier of war.

After a long, gruelling trek through the Carpathian Mountains, the soldiers made camp just beyond the castle walls. They pitched their tents in the fading light, kindled fires, and began preparing their evening meal. The camp came alive with activity: cooks boiled hearty soups over open flames, skinned a freshly hunted deer, and chopped vegetables with practiced hands. Around them, other soldiers sharpened their swords, polished their muskets, and carried out various duties, keeping the unit humming with quiet efficiency and purpose.

Smith admired the massive size of Castle Cachtice and how well-kept the grounds were. He also noticed a strange funeral procession with three wooden caskets carted into a nearby cemetery, followed by Pastor Istivan.

"Three deaths? One funeral?" John Smith questioned.

"Be mindful around these parts, Mr. Smith," the Earl of Meldritch said. "The Lord Nadasdy and Countess Bathory are the Lords of these lands and answer to nobody but the king.

They would not second-guess killing you or me. They are too valuable to the crown, bringing the Holy Roman Emperor millions in taxes. Safe to say that the Nadasdy-Bathory family funds most of the Holy Roman Empire and, as a result, are untouchable."

"I see," John Smith said.

"Those three caskets may be for thieves, or disorderlies," the Earl followed.

"I shall be on my absolute best behaviour," Smith said slyly.

The Earl and Smith shared a laugh as the sun set over the horizon, casting a brilliant red sky overhead.

Ferenc Nadasdy greeted all his servants in the lavish castle, including the high-ranking Helena, Illona, Dorka, and Fitzko. It had been almost a year since he had seen their faces, and he was genuinely happy for their company.

"Welcome home, my Lord," Dorka said, giving a curtsy.

"So glad you've returned," Helena added.

"It has been too long. Let us prepare a feast for us and our new guests!" Ferenc yelled in the grand hall of the castle.

"Yes, my Lord," Illona said, as she immediately started deliberating tasks and assigning various duties amongst the dozens of servants.

Inside her bedroom chamber, Elizabeth Bathory had waited for Ferenc after nearly a year without seeing him. She slowly emerged and walked down the tower steps, dressed in a stunning black dress that captivated the Black Knight of Hungary. Ferenc watched her every step as she came toward him.

"My Lady," Ferenc said to Elizabeth.

"My Lord," Elizabeth said. "It has been ages since I have seen your Grace."

"I have missed you wholeheartedly," Ferenc said as they embraced with a kiss.

"Are you home for good?" Elizabeth asked. "Tell me the war has finally ended."

"I wish I could say so, my dearest. I am here only for a couple of nights, unfortunately. The Habsburgs have hired thousands of mercenaries to help us defeat the Turks. We depart for Castle Sarvar the day after next," Ferenc said.

"I had hoped for more than a couple of nights," Elizabeth said, whispering and kissing Ferenc's neck.

"Come, show me to your study. I have something to show you," Ferenc said, grabbing Elizabeth around the waist and guiding her up the stairs.

The two entered the chamber and closed the door, where their passions took hold. They both removed their clothes, layer upon layer. Ferenc threw his wife on the bed and then himself upon the skinny, frail Elizabeth. He took nips at her flesh, up and down her neck and breasts. Though his bites did not draw blood, Elizabeth still relished the pain.

Ferenc and Elizabeth made rough passionate love. It was hasty, graceless, and inelegant after months without each other's rhythms and intimacies. Ferenc's breathing was deep and loud. His legs bothered him throughout the reunion, which did not last long as he finished on top of Elizabeth, who smiled with delight at providing her husband pleasure.

Elizabeth was growing increasingly uncertain of herself. She believed her looks were fading, and soon she wouldn't be able to satisfy her husband. But on this occasion, she felt beautiful, refined, and necessary as Ferenc finished with sweat and heavy breath.

"It is so good to see you again," Ferenc said, lying beside Elizabeth. "I have a special present for you."

"Do you?"

Ferenc rolled over and reached for his satchel, removing a small cloth bag. "I found this on my travels to Prague. It's quite ingenious," he said.

Elizabeth opened the bag and found what resembled a large metal hand. It had sharp metal claws and spikes around the knuckles. Elizabeth slipped her hand inside the metal glove and displayed the obscure weapon to her husband.

"I love it," Elizabeth said with a smile.

"The merchant called it a raker," Ferenc said with a cheeky smile.

"A raker?"

"A raker, indeed," Ferenc affirmed.

"It is so scary," Elizabeth said with a smile.

"I knew you would love it," Ferenc said, kissing his naked wife.

"Husband, on another topic, I forgot to inform you that we have a Greek, Latin, and English teacher coming to start tutoring our dear boy, Paul," Elizabeth said. "Peter Dowling is his name, and his daughter accompanies him."

"Well, terrific. I assume we have arranged separate quarters for them?" Ferenc inquired.

"They have rooms across from one another in the south wing," Elizabeth responded.

"What about Kata and Anna? Have you heard word from our daughters?" Ferenc asked.

"They both send the occasional letter. By the sounds of things, they are not sure of what love is yet," Elizabeth said with a smile.

"They will soon learn," Ferenc said, rolling his naked body back on top of his wife.

Outside the massive limestone castle walls, John Smith and the rest of the regiment watched solemnly as funeral hymns echoed through the air.

Workers lowered one casket into the ground while they prepared another for burial. Smith had never witnessed a funeral for more than one person outside of a soldier's funeral, and the sight unsettled him. The sights, the sounds, and the quiet routine all struck him as strange, almost surreal. The moment revealed the dark nature surrounding Transylvania and Hungary, leaving Smith with a lingering sense of unease.

"What do you suppose happened, Thomas?" John asked his fellow English soldier.

"Well, plague and cholera are spreading throughout Europe. "They may have taken a hard hit here," Thomas replied. "They close the caskets to stop fear from spreading."

"Hmm. It all seems odd; three funerals at night. Closed caskets and all," John said.

"Have you ever seen someone dying of the plague?" Thomas asked.

"No, I have not," John responded.

"It is gruesome in the most nauseating way, Mr. Smith," Thomas said. "The pus and the blood ooze from the skin."

"Good God," Smith said.

That evening, after the funerals, the castle seemed to come alive for the first time in months. Laughter and music filled the courtyard, the smell of cooking wafted through the halls, and a campfire illuminated the walls of Castle Cachtice. The Count and Countess felt they were newlyweds, drinking wine and feeling rosy-cheeked merriment.

The grand hall was filled with noblemen and women, including the Earl of Meldritch and Elizabeth's cousin George Thurzo, who had travelled to Cachtice to help guide the soldiers to the Danube River. Hundreds of candles burned, music played, and servants topped everyone's wine glasses.

"I would like to propose a toast!" Ferenc said, standing up. "Thank you to the Earl of Meldritch for guiding our new soldiers through the Carpathians. And thank you to Count George Thurzo for looking after my family in my extended absences from home. Now, we march together and put an end to Mehmed III and his barbaric hordes."

All of the guests cheered and yelled, "Here, here!"

"And to my beloved, beautiful wife!" Ferenc said as he stood at the head of the table. "To her gracefulness, beauty, and administrative qualities in my absence. She is irreplaceable. She is my world. Now raise your glasses to my love, your hostess, Countess Bathory. May God bless and protect her!"

Elizabeth smiled, feeling a surge of joy and pride run through her body for the first time in months.

Chapter 10 - The Sheppard and his Flock

In the small village of Cachtice, a few miles from the castle, peasants worked hard raising animals, sowing crops, and forging iron for Nadasdy, Bathory, and their surrounding empire. Elizabeth, on occasion, would frequent the village to attend mass at the church in the centre of town; otherwise, she would have no reason to be there.

Though the Countess and her iron fist ruled the villagers, they found small pleasures in life, despite the dangers and their abject poverty. Church was a focal point in their livelihood, as they sang hymns, performed Catholic traditions, and gave thanks for all they had.

Pastor Istivan led congregations at the small, humble church. He was growing more and more concerned with the number of deaths happening at Castle Cachtice, but he knew he had to be careful about his words and actions. Families had been reaching out and pleading for their daughters to return, but Istivan was helpless against the power of Bathory and Nadasdy.

The Sunday mass poured into the church, ready to hear the Lord's good word. People of all ages came in from the cool spring morning and filled the wooden pews. The space was warm and inviting as the trustworthy, humble Pastor Istivan took to the podium.

"A month from now, we will celebrate the feast of St. George, a man whose name has become synonymous with bravery, faith, and the triumph of good over evil. St. George is remembered as a valiant soldier and a martyr who stood firm in his commitment to Christ, even in the face of death. His story inspires us to remain steadfast in our faith, even when called to make great sacrifices," Pastor Istivan began.

In one of the back rows of the church sat a young family of four. The Kovacs family were peasants, but were happy and excited for the spring ahead. Jan and Catharine parents, of Maria and Sam, listened attentively to Pastor Istivan's sermon. Maria was a young teenager who had worn her best dress for the Sunday occasion. Sam was just a little boy who sat bored, but well-behaved in between his mother and father.

Pastor Istivan continued his eulogy: "I want to speak further on St. George as I feel he deserves more than one Sunday sermon yearly. St. George's conviction in the love of God was unwavering, and he boldly professed his belief, even though it led to his torture and eventual martyrdom. Executed for his witness to the Almighty, St. George did not die in vain. His courage and faith became a beacon of hope for all Christians, Catholic or Protestant."

A young man named Michael Gorzi came through the church doors. Still a teenager, Michael was a grown, handsome boy with slicked-back hair for the Sunday occasion. The young man peered around, saw the Kovacs family, and quietly sat down at the end of the pew.

"St. George's courage was not in slaying dragons or defeating enemies with a sword, but in his faith and willingness to suffer for truth's sake. He stood for Christ when it was not easy to do so, and he was willing to endure great hardship to protect the Christian faith," Pastor Istivan said.

Michael peered down the pew at Maria, who glanced back with a smile. The two teenagers were clearly familiar with each other. Little Sam looked at Michael and stuck out his tiny tongue.

"In a world that often tells us to be silent about our beliefs or to compromise, we must ask ourselves: are we willing to stand up for what we believe? Are we ready to serve others? Are we ready to protect the innocent and fight for justice? Finally, the story of St. George reminds us of the ultimate victory of good over all evil. No matter what dragons we face in our lives, whether they are doubts, fears, or evil people, we can take comfort in the fact that, through God, we have already won the ultimate victory."

As little Sam continued sticking his tongue out at the newly arrived Michael, Maria gave him a subtle wink, making Michael's heart skip a beat. Michael loved Maria and doted on her every word. They had known each other since they were five and were inseparable.

"As we remember St. George, let us pray that his example of faith, courage, and service may inspire us to live more fully and have the strength to face the challenges in our lives. Now, let us pray: O God, who gave St. George to your church as a model of courage and faith, grant that we may follow his example of steadfastness in faith and in service to you. May his witness inspire us to live more boldly as Christians, and may we have the strength to face all life's challenges with the conviction of your love. Through Christ our Lord. Amen."

The entire congregation followed: "Amen."

After the sermon, everyone gave their tributes and made their way home. Though it was Sunday, the Kovacs still had much to do around their farmland.

Jan, Catharine, and their children walked along the muddy road to their wood and mud home with thatched roofing. It was a two-room home and was functional and straightforward. Inside was a central fireplace and simple, functional furniture.

Catharine put on a pot of water and began preparing dinner. At the same time, Jan went to tend the goats and pigs they kept outside, though occasionally, the animals would sleep inside the house during frigid temperatures.

Sam followed his father outside, while Maria changed out of her dress and put it inside the lone wooden chest in the bedroom. Two large straw-stuffed mattresses were in the bedroom, with a few, half-burned candles.

"Maria, come help me cut and peel some potatoes," Catharine yelled from the other room.

"Yes, mother," Maria responded.

Maria joined her mother and began washing and peeling the potatoes. Potatoes were a relatively new crop in Eastern Europe, as Sir Walter Raleigh had brought them from the Americas a decade before. At first, they were not very popular, but they were easy to grow, rich in nutrients, and became more of a staple in the diets of Europeans.

"I saw Michael at church today," Catharine said, smiling.

"Oh, really?" Maria responded, playing dumb.

Catharine knew Maria and Michael were in young love. She had a similar experience with a young Jan. There was a knock on the door. "Oh, that must be him," Catharine said.

"Who?" Maria questioned.

"Michael. I've invited him for dinner," Catharine answered.

"What!"

Catharine opened the door to a young Michael carrying a loaf of bread.

"Hello, Mrs. Kovacs. I have brought a fresh loaf of bread," Michael said with a grin.

Catharine looked at Maria, smiling at Michael. "Please, come in, Michael," the proud mother said.

Michael was strong, healthy, pure of heart, and obviously taken with young Maria. He never missed an opportunity to see her. Catharine and Jan knew Maria would need to marry soon in a tumultuous world filled with sickness and violence.

Michael was the son of a hemp farmer who provided the Bathory-Nadasdy estates with vast amounts of the crop. Hemp was used in everything from clothes to paper to make rope and weave baskets. It was also occasionally smoked by people seeking relief from the day's hardships. Michael and his family worked tirelessly to keep the Count and Countess happy.

That evening, the Kovacs family and Michael shared a filling meal and gave thanks and prayed for a successful crop in the coming months.

—William Mowat—

Chapter 11 - A Grand Tour

Peter Dowling and his daughter Margaret arrived at the Royal Palace of Prague and walked through its grand halls, admiring all the sculptures and paintings. Jacob Strada, the curator of Rudolph's grand collection, guided them. Having read the works of Sophocles, Aristotle, and Euripides, Peter was mesmerized by the ancient marble reliefs from ancient Greece. He paused in front of a marble sarcophagus that depicted the battle of the Amazons.

"Margaret, do you recognize this relief sculpture?" Peter asked his daughter.

"It reminds me of the Parthenon frieze at the Acropolis. Is this the battle of the Amazons versus the Greeks?" Margaret asked, putting her hand on her chin.

"Correct, my dear," Peter said. "Who is this?"

Margaret looked at the marble statue and immediately recognized the ancient female. "That's easy. Athena, goddess of courage and justice, daughter of Zeus."

"Excellent," Peter said.

"Athena Nike!" Margaret added enthusiastically.

"Well done, my dear," Peter responded. Peter closely inspected and appreciated the fine detail of the sculpture, and could not help but feel like a little child. He imagined himself on Mount Olympus, high in the clouds, basking in the sun, wearing a white toga with the rest of the deities.

Peter and Margaret were having the time of their life. It had been a long two months, sailing from London to Venice and then a horse and wagon ride from Venice to Prague, but they were both in great spirits to be in such a cultured, foreign place, with comfortable accommodations.

Peter was extremely proud of his daughter. The only thing that she had complained about was the rats on the boat from London to Venice. She was a dreamer and was constantly searching for knowledge.

"This is a highly polished steel mirror, constructed by Pythagoras, a Greek mathematician. It is said to have been made for divination, at around 500 B.C. Just like our Emperor Rudolph, even the ancients were searching for the divine by supernatural means." Strada enjoyed his job as both tour guide and curator. Few people got to see the collection, so when he had the chance to boast, he did not hesitate.

"Incredible piece," Peter said.

"Mirrors like this were created at the full moon, for divination. Diviners by mirrors were called Specularii by the Romans. They used them to learn about the issue of battles at the time. Hard to say how accurate they were," Strada said with a little chuckle.

Strada guided them into the strange oddities room. Although Strada was a wise man, con artists often duped him. He paid exorbitant amounts of gold for mythical specimens that he believed were rare and priceless.

"These are the teeth of a mermaid captured in the Aegean sea," Strada said, pointing to a small glass case.

Margaret glanced at her father with a look of disbelief.

"And here we have the feathers of a phoenix, witnessed by Maximillian in 1313 A.D."

"Isn't the phoenix a mythical creature?" Margaret asked.

"Nothing is certain, my dear," Strada said, continuing to move through the room. "Here is a prized possession from Jerusalem; two nails from Noah's ark."

"Interesting," Peter said in a highly suspicious tone. "I always wondered where his ship landed."

Margaret chuckled, as Strada did not catch on to Peter's sarcasm.

"These are the rare scales of a dragon," Strada said, pointing to another small case. "They are said to have come from the dragon that Saint George the divine killed," Strada said, admiring the specimen.

Though nobody had seen a dragon before, it was hard to dispute the massive Tyrannosaurus Rex skull on display.

"Could there be real dragons?" Margaret asked.

"St. George would certainly say so," Strada said, smiling at Margaret.

"I couldn't say whether dragons are real, but this is a massive lizard-like animal. Maybe 30-40 feet tall. The teeth indicate it was likely a meat-eater. Quite remarkable. Massive nasal cavity. I would love to see the entire skeletal specimen," Peter said. "Where did you find this?"

"I believe it was acquired from a Spanish trader who claimed to have retrieved it from the Americas," Strada said.

"So much of the world is still so puzzling and undiscovered," Peter said, closely inspecting the skull.

"Let us continue," Strada said. "The Emperor is a lover of stones, and not simply because he hopes thus to increase his dignity and majesty, but through them to raise awareness of the glory of God. That is to say that the beauty of the whole world is in such small bodies and in them, unites the seeds of all other things in creation."

"Beautifully said, Mr. Strada," Peter said.

"What's that?" Margaret said, pointing at a peculiar device atop a tripod.

"That is one of the earliest refracting telescopes developed by Leonard Diggs. Our own court mathematician, Johannes Kepler, continues to develop a new model," Strada said.

"Does Kepler believe in the heliocentric conception of the universe?" Peter asked.

"He does share the heliocentric conception with Copernicus, which has been a remarkable discovery and changed our entire outlook on the universe," Strada answered.

"Heliocentric? Helios, Greek for sun?" Margaret asked.

"Very good, my dear. Do you know the Greek language?" Strada asked.

"My father has taught me some Latin and Greek, but I'm still learning," Margaret answered.

"Excellent, well, we are glad to employ such a scholarly language arts teacher. Rudolf has summoned many great historians, antiquarians, mathematicians, astronomers, and expert theologians. Many great physicians and alchemists have also come to Prague," Strada said.

"My daughter and I are humbled by your invitation and hospitality, my Lord. We are forever grateful," Peter said.

Strada smiled as he guided them through the massive rooms full of art collections, scientific instruments, astronomy devices, musical instruments, and finally approached the royal throne room.

"The Emperor has just finished construction on the Cathedral of St. George, just there, across from the convent, where the nuns used to elect the Queens of ancient Bohemia," Strada said.

Peter and Margaret peered through the window at a beautiful new church with twin towers and carefully landscaped gardens.

"Gorgeous landscaping, my Lord," Margaret said, admiring the blooming gardens.

"King Rudolph's royal collection is admired throughout Europe," Strada said, opening the doors to the royal throne room. "You are two of the lucky few who get to witness the collection firsthand."

The Holy Roman Emperor Rudolph II sat inside with his black jacket and truffled collar. Dressed in lavish imperial garments, Rudolph sat in an armchair with his knees crossed. A royally appointed artist painted the Emperor with a stolid face, exhibiting neither happiness, curiosity, nor astonishment. Rudolph sat in front of a group of ladies and gentlemen of the court. A lady was leaning forward, trying to keep a surprised look on her face as she looked at a stuffed platypus. Behind him stood a group of courtiers, dressed in doublets, white leg hose, high-heeled, and low-cut shoes. Each held a sword in a different position.

The whole spectacle caught Peter and Margaret off guard. They stood in awe of the scene before them.

"Our King is extremely busy," Strada told Peter and Margaret.

"Of course, Lord Strada," Peter responded.

"Today, we've arranged a painting of the King and his holy courtiers depicting his Majesty's keen interest in the sciences and his commitment towards knowledge," Strada described.

"What is that?" Margaret said, pointing.

"That is a platypus, my dear," Strada said. "One of the unique animals collected from the far reaches of the globe. Though it is classified as a mammal, it curiously lays eggs."

"We also saw the lion and tiger in the courtyard," Margaret said. "Dangerous animals to be left roaming."

"We have many exotic animals like elephants, apes, lions, tigers, and birds of every shape and colour you can imagine," Strada said. "The Emperor insists on allowing Mohammed, the lion, to roam free. He was a gift from the Turkish Sultan many years ago. There have only been minor attacks, nothing fatal," Strada said, smiling.

"The Emperor sure loves animals, doesn't he?" Margaret asked.

"If he cannot have a live specimen, he will consider a stuffed version; if a stuffed version is not available, he will have a royal artist paint a picture of the species," Strada said. "So, yes indeed, the Emperor does love animals, my dear."

"Spectacular," Peter said in awe of the scene before him.

Strada approached Emperor Rudolph. "Your Majesty, this is Mr. Peter Dowling. He has agreed to teach and tutor English, Greek, and Latin under your Holy leadership."

Rudolph did his best to remain a statue. "Welcome, Mr. Dowling."

"Thank you, my Lord," Peter said.

"Who is this?" Rudolph asked.

"This is my daughter, Margaret, my Lord," Peter answered.

"Margaret, my dear, welcome to Prague. Are you enjoying the royal tour of my collection and cabinets of curiosities?" Rudolph asked.

"It has been marvellous, my Lord," Margaret answered.

"Peter and Margaret have travelled from London to be here, my King," Strada said.

"England! That is terrific. I am so happy for your Queen Elizabeth and her clever tactics in defeating King Philip II. While I was tutored in his royal court, I never really did enjoy his company," Rudolph joked.

Strada was the only one to laugh. Peter and Margaret only smiled at the King's humour.

"You were schooled with King Philip?" Margaret asked.

"Indeed, my dear. Philip was my uncle. My mother and Philip were brother and sister. He and I are both royal Habsburgs. I spent much of my life living at the Spanish court; it wasn't a fond memory. Did you know my uncle Philip was once married to Mary Tudor, the Queen of England, before her sister Elizabeth became ruler? So, you see, it is a small world, and England is very dear to my heart."

"Sorry to hear of Philip's passing. I suppose Philip III will be the next great Spanish King," Peter said.

"Philip III is wise, pleasant, and respectful," Rudolph said. "I am sure he will do a terrific job. Does your Queen of England have a successor?"

"We Britons love our aged Queen," Peter said. "But, there is no clear successor at this point."

"Elizabeth, the daughter of Henry VIII; my father despised that fat, conceited man," Rudolph said.

"Elizabeth is the last of the Tudors, and the Stuarts may reign again," Peter said.

"Are you referring to the only son of Mary, Queen of Scots, the headless conspirator?" Rudolph questioned, as he gave a subtle laugh.

"She comes from a long line, leading back to Robert the Bruce, King of Scots," Peter said.

"Fascinating, Mr. Dowling. England has entered such an exciting time in its long history," Rudolph said.

"Indeed, my Lord," Peter said.

"I am sure you are familiar with William Shakespeare's plays. Have you had the opportunity to see any of them?" he asked. "We here in Prague are all quite jealous of such rich, poetic work presented in such a valiant, accessible manner."

"Before our journey here to the Royal Palace, Margaret and I had the opportunity to watch a performance of Julius Caesar at the newly constructed Globe Theatre," Peter answered.

"Tell me more, Mr. Dowling," Rudolph asked.

"His prose and intelligence are like no other, my Lord. The audience, myself included, invests in his characters as they navigate through an array of emotions and a world full of obstacles. Last summer Margaret and I saw A Midsummer Night's Dream, and were transported to a world full of fairies, magic, love, humour, and ancient traditions."

"It must have been wonderful," Rudolph said. "I have sent many offers to Shakespeare; however, I have yet to hear a formal response."

"At the end of Julius Caesar, Shakespeare appeared during the curtain call to a rousing ovation," Peter answered. "Even the Queen adores Shakespeare's prose. The ovations and applause he receives are like nothing else."

"Remarkable," Rudolph said.

"Mr. Dowling is a grammar school teacher in London, my Liege. Our staffing committee believes his strengths in Latin and Greek, combined with his sound knowledge of the English language, would make him an ideal candidate for Castle Cachtice and the tutelage for the Count and Countess," Strada said.

"He sounds like an excellent fit for the Nadasdy-Bathory family. Give him a contract with a signing bonus of 500 gold pieces," Rudolph said. "Does that sound reasonable, Mr. Dowling?"

"Most reasonable, my Lord," Peter responded, giving a thankful bow to the King.

Peter was ecstatic inside. His head filled with joy, and his body tingled at the thought of wealth. He felt a lifetime of stress roll off his shoulders. He was finally financially stable and could purchase land and ensure his daughter would have a dowry.

"Wonderful, Mr. Dowling. We are pleased to have you in our Kingdom. Mr. Strada will arrange payment, transportation, and accommodations for the duration of your visit. Should you need anything else, Mr. Dowling, do not hesitate to ask," Rudolph said.

"Thank you, most cordially, my Liege," Peter said.

"Thank you for your commitment to the Holy Roman Empire," Rudolph said. "It was a pleasure to meet you, Margaret."

"My sincerest gratitude for a tour of your esteemed collection, your Majesty. I shall forever remember this kind, pleasurable visit," Margaret said.

"It was my pleasure, my dear," Rudolph said.

Strada led Peter and Margaret out of the throne room. Later that evening, Strada secured the contract and 500 pieces of gold for Peter and his daughter, which was a small fortune for them. The Dowlings stayed a few more nights in Prague and eventually departed for Castle Cachtice, deep in the foggy Carpathian Mountains.

Chapter 12 - A Tale of Youth

Elizabeth Bathory sat on a wooden stool in the dimly lit chamber of her dungeon. A few dead bodies lay before her, and another hung by her ankles as blood drained from her lifeless body into a wooden barrel.

There was only one living girl in the room. She was barely conscious, chained, and had cuts all over her naked body, from her ankles all the way up to her face. The Countess had been slowly torturing the girl. The helpless girl screamed with each slice, fuelling Elizabeth's desire to continue.

"Your screams are like music to my ears," the Countess said.

"Please, my Lady," the girl said, as she wept tears on the cold stone floor.

"When I was just a little girl, no older than seven, I was first introduced to this world of discipline," Elizabeth coldly said. "At my uncle's royal castle in Poland, a man had stolen from a local merchant, a simple loaf of bread or something along those lines. My uncle and his men rounded him up and put him in a cell, much like this one. Then, my Uncle Bathory brought me down and showed me what happened to thieves like this in his kingdom, as if he knew that I would one day rule, and this was how rulers ruled."

The cold, shivering girl could only listen to Elizabeth's story, as she knew Bathory could snap at any time and end her life.

"The scraggly thief was dragged by whip and lash into a neighbouring farmer's field outside the castle walls. Not knowing what was about to happen, my heart began to race with anxious uncertainty; it was all so exciting. My uncle's guards viciously broke the man's arms and legs with wooden clubs, to prevent escape, you see. Then, my uncle's men brought the man before a rotting, putrid, decomposing dead horse. The thief was squashed and crudely sewn into the belly of the carcass and left with only his head exposed. Day and night, jackals, wild dogs, ravens, crows, and vultures pestered the thief."

The pale, bloody girl continued to listen to Elizabeth without moving a muscle.

"The stench was revolting; I could hardly bear it. I remember my eyes watering and feeling my stomach heave. The man slowly starved to death, and each day, I would venture to the field and look at the dead man. The scene told a lasting, poetic story that stayed with me. I felt no sorrow, nor empathy for the peasant thief. My uncle reassured me that we were creating a glorious kingdom that would not tolerate thieves or crimes of any sort. He said I might have to issue such orders one day, and that I would need to rule with an iron fist. In our kingdom, thieves and criminals would be expendable; only the strongest, most obedient peasants would survive. Early in my youth, my family instilled this lesson: I am the ruler of this castle and these lands. I rule with an iron fist."

Elizabeth cut the girl's face and bare shoulder as she let out a harrowing scream.

"Cry as loud as you like. There is not a soul on earth that is coming to save you," Elizabeth said, smiling.

Outside the closed cell door sat the dwarf servant Fitzko, who was all too excited by the sounds of screams and laughter. Fitzko had been at Elizabeth's side for nearly a decade and took great pride in doing her bidding. He would kidnap girls from neighbouring villages at her request and would trick others with promises of arranged marriage, money, fame, or prestigious education.

Authorities never questioned Elizabeth's actions, mainly because her noble status placed her above the law. For members of the high aristocracy like Elizabeth and Ferenc, killing peasants was not considered a crime. Their social rank granted them immunity from prosecution. Moreover, any potential scrutiny was deflected by the surrounding chaos. The outbreak of the plague and the spread of other deadly diseases also distracted officials and crippled meaningful investigation.

Girls, unknowingly, came from all around Hungary to have the opportunity to be trained in a courtly, noble manner. Most girls whom Elizabeth tortured went to the castle willingly with promises of nobility, such as an arranged marriage with a high-ranking official. Fitzko had become an expert trickster and was at the heart of recruiting the girls.

Elizabeth came barging through the cell door and startled the sitting Fitzko. "Dispose of the body, immediately. I'm tired of the screams," she said, handing the bloody knife to Fitzko.

The dwarf peered inside the cell to see the girl hanging by her wrists, with her throat slit.

"I will be back after dinner," Elizabeth said. "Also, clean up the blood, Fitzko."

"Yes, your Grace," Fitzko said with a bow.

Elizabeth left up the stairs, while Fitzko obtained the help of Helena, Dorka, and Illona. Together, the four trusted servants of Bathory moved two dead bodies up the steps and out to the courtyard. Night had fallen, as they discreetly threw the naked, sliced-up bodies over the castle wall down to the cold, muddy ground below. The bodies landed with unsettling thuds that put even Fitzko off.

Pieces of other bodies were strewn across the ground below, torn apart by the Carpathian wolves and other roaming animals. The bodies of victims were piling up so fast that they didn't have the time or energy to continue to bury the bodies and have priests come to give the funeral rites. Elizabeth's cruel desire for blood showed no signs of slowing down.

"The Cachtice priest grows suspicious of this place," Fitzko said.

"He will do nothing," Illona said, with a violent tone.

Pastor Istivan in the village of Cachtice had become increasingly suspicious over the past few months, as local girls continued to go missing. Dozens of reports landed on his desk about missing daughters and sisters. The Pastor knew he could never directly accuse the Countess of her wrongdoings, because she could have him killed without question. So, Pastor Istivan consulted with the high priests of Hungary. To no avail, the holy council urged him to keep quiet, as the Nadasdy-Bathory family was too powerful and vital to feeding the congregations across Hungary.

"The Count and Countess are untouchable," Helena said, peering down at the pile of bodies.

Helena had been teaching the Countess several new ways to torture victims, stemming from ancient texts and legends that she was constantly researching. Thought to be a witch by many, Helena made horrible poisons and potions; she inflicted diseases on people, spoiled crops, brought harsh weather, and performed the devil's work. When other castle servants saw Helena, they didn't say a word and often avoided her altogether. The real threat of being cursed loomed throughout the castle.

"Ashes to ashes, dust to dust," Helena began a funeral chant. "Thy soul departs; in ether it must. By the moon's pale light, by the sun's warm kiss, we say farewell to this mortal bliss. Come forth, O shadows, guide the way, and carry the soul where it may lie. By blood and bone, by flame and stone, thy journey's end is now thy own," Helena coldly said. As she stared down at the bodies below, a pack of wolves, in the distance, began howling under the full blood moon.

—William Mowat—

Chapter 13 - The Three Turks

Ferenc Nadasdy, the Earl of Meldritch, and John Smith had fought a few bloody battles together. John had begun to lead the cavalry into major victories along the Danube River against the Muslim armies of the Ottoman Empire.

Meldritch, Nadasdy, and Smith led an army of eight thousand men toward the heavily fortified mountain city of Regall. Defended by Turks, Tatars, and renegades from the surrounding lands of Zarkam, Regall was a formidable stronghold. Even securing the valley below required the strategic ingenuity of the three commanders. Unfortunately for the Earl, the operation took longer than anticipated. He had to delay the assault, which gave the enemy six crucial days to prepare for the impending siege.

The Ottomans called in all the surrounding animals and supplies, mobilized all the forces, and set traps around the city's exterior. Both sides dug trenches and lay waiting. The Turkish troops were not convinced that the Earl of Meldritch, the Black Knight of Hungary, and their small army could take the city.

Meldritch had dozens of cannons, which would cause havoc for the Turks, and reinforcements were on their way. Meldritch only needed to wait.

"You Christians will grow too fat for just using cannons!" one Turk yelled to the besiegers. "Come fight!"

"Go away!" another Turk yelled.

"Don't go away without giving us a fight!" the Turkish captain said, as everyone laughed.

As both armies waited, a Turkish messenger delivered a message to Lord Nadasdy.

"Did you invite us for dinner?" Ferenc joked as he took the paper letter from the messenger. He opened the letter and read: *"That to delight the ladies of our great city, and to show our great Lord Turbashaw who is the best among us, let us see who will fight against our best warrior, and risk losing their head."*

Ferenc laughed and brought the message before the Earl of Meldritch, and after some discussion, they agreed to send a Christian warrior to battle the Turkish champion. They drew straws, and by chance, John Smith's name was chosen to fight the Turk.

Young and full of pomp and pride, John Smith was more than willing to risk his life to defeat the enemy, no matter what the setting or rules were. He had been training his whole life for this moment to showcase his skill as a rider and swordsman.

The following day, with spectators on both sides able to observe, the trumpets sounded and the Turkish champion rode onto the field. Mounted on a massive black stallion, he carried a joust and a shield. He had two wings of eagle feathers set in precious stones, and gold protruded from his shoulders.

The second set of trumpets ushered in John Smith. Now only 21 years old, but having the experience of a military veteran, an able seaman, and an expert strategist, Smith rode out to meet his foe. John's entrance was much simpler and more humble than his opponent's. His breath and nerves are steady as he focuses solely on his enemy.

Moments later, the horn sounded, and the two riders immediately rode towards each other. Smith and the Turk raised their lances, leaving dust trails in their wake.

"For Turbashaw!" the Turk yelled.

John Smith let out a massive battle cry as his lance pierced through the Turk's neck. Smith's lance shattered into pieces as the Turkish warrior's head and torso slouched over, and he eventually fell from the horse. In accordance with the terms agreed upon, Smith dismounted his horse, removed the helmet from his dead opponent, and cut his head off with his drawn, freshly-sharpened sword.

As the head rolled away from Turk's body, the crowd moaned in disgust at the gruesome sight. Smith picked up the head of his fallen foe and brought it to Lord Nadasdy and the Earl of Meldritch. The whole army cheered for Smith as he paraded the trophy along the ranks of his fellow soldiers.

The janissaries in the Turkish camp stirred and were clearly shocked at what had just transpired. A giant man emerged from the crowded street and approached the Turbashaw at his lavish tent.

"Who might you be?" the bearded Turbashaw asked.

"I am Grualgo, friend to our fallen Turk. I seek revenge, my Lord Turbashaw," Grualgo said in his deep voice.

Turbashaw paused as he stared at Grualgo, looking for signs of insincerity. "I shall arrange for your revenge, Grualgo," Turbashaw said as he nodded in affirmation. Turbashaw rose from his chair and made his way to the battlefield. Ferenc Nadasdy and the Earl of Meldritch greeted the Turkish leader under a banner of truce.

"How now, wise Lord Turbashaw," Nadasdy said. "Coming for your friend's head?"

Meldritch smiled at Ferenc's comment.

"I have an upset young man who is seeking revenge for his fallen friend," Turbashaw innocently said. "His name is Grualgo, and he seeks a new challenge with your John Smith. Grualgo will offer his horse and armour to Smith if defeated; if Grualgo wins, he will reclaim his friend's head."

Nadasdy and Meldritch consulted and agreed with the Turkish leader's proposal.

"Tomorrow, your warrior will have his chance at redemption," Nadasdy said, knowing John Smith would agree in a heartbeat.

"Tomorrow then," Turbashaw said.

The next day, the second round of jousting began. Smith and Grualgo faced each other as they mounted their horses and were handed their joust and shield. The trumpets sounded, and the riders rode towards one another. Completing pass after pass, the lances eventually shred into splinters. Both men then draw their pistols and charge the next pass. Smith took a bullet to the chest plate but was unaffected by the shot. Smith rose from being hit and fired his pistol at the charging Grualgo. The Turk caught the bullet in the shoulder and fell violently from his horse. Smith turned about and saw the lifeless Grualgo lying on the ground. Smith dismounted his horse, drew his sword, and carefully approached the Turk.

The Christian army cheered as the Turkish crowds fell silent.

"I shall do what was promised," Smith said, as he swung his sword. Grualgo's head rolled from his body, and the crowd erupted in applause. Smith also removed the armour from his body and grabbed the Turkish horse by the reins.

Smith then slowly walked back into the Christian camp carrying his new prizes.

The next day, Smith woke feeling elated from the support he was getting from his army. His valiant nature led him to show the Turks that the Christians were just as chivalrous as themselves. Early after sunrise, he rode his new Turkish horse and yelled to the lines of the Ottoman city: "If any of you Turks want your friend's heads back, and want to redeem their honour, you now have the chance!"

A giant man yelled from the city wall. "I challenge you!"

"Who says?" John yelled back.

"Bonny Mulgro says!" the giant said, walking to meet the challenger. "But we do not fight on horses or with lances."

"What say you, then, Bonny Mulgro?" Smith asked.

"Battle-axes," Mulgro answered.

"Pistols?" Smith replied.

"Sure," Mulgro said, nodding.

It did not take long before the two faced each other on the battlefield. Again, the crowds gathered to see the hand-to-hand entertainment. The two pulled their pistols and fired without any harm, then charged each other with raised axes. Mulgro was mighty in his swings, while Smith did his best to avoid the ferocious blows. One of Mulgro's overhead swings landed in the ground as Smith dodged and saw his opportunity.

With a mighty blow, Smith viciously swung his axe and sent Mulgro's head flying in the air. Blood spilled all over the dusty ground, and the crowd groaned at the grisly sight.

That evening, a grand reception was held in Smith's honour. He arrived at the general's pavilion with three newly acquired horses and three swords. Smith's procession followed behind him, carrying three lances with the heads of his fallen challengers.

Stephen Bathory, Prince of Transylvania, and Elizabeth Bathory's uncle, came to grant official knighthood to John Smith. Bathory had officially joined the Holy League and married Maria Christina of Habsburg, a niece of the Holy Roman Emperor, Rudolph II. Stephen Bathory was nearly 70 years old and did not go near battlefields; however, he was partial to ceremony and feasts. He was also the family member who taught Elizabeth how to torture and condition her people to be obedient citizens.

Elizabeth Bathory's cousin, Count George Thurzo, a new commander and high-ranking official in the Hungarian army, accompanied Stephen Bathory. All of the Hungarian-Transylvanian leadership had shown up to pay homage to a fearless, honourable Christian warrior whose story had spread quickly.

In recognition of his bravery and service, the Earl of Meldritch formally gave John Smith the rank of Captain and a generous reward of 500 gold pieces. The honours, bestowed during a grand reception, was attended by nobles, military officers, and dignitaries from afar. The ceremony climaxed with the unveiling of Captain Smith's newly granted coat of arms. The richly adorned shield, presented with ceremonial fanfare, bore a striking and grim emblem: the severed heads of three Turks, a bold symbol of Smith's valour in combat against the Ottoman forces.

"All hail for our champion, Captain John Smith, the great beheader of Turks!" Meldritch announced as the 8000 men cheered for the young man.

"I shall don this shield with great pride, my Lord," Smith said to Meldritch.

"You have done me proud, Captain," Meldritch said, extending his hand.

"Thank you for having faith in me, your Grace," Captain John Smith said, shaking the Earl's hand.

There were handshakes all around, including Ferenc Nadasdy. "Congratulations, Captain Smith," Ferenc said. "You certainly have earned your shield today."

It had been a long few months on the various battlefields in the Carpathian Mountains. Ferenc Nadasdy's legs were causing him tremendous pain, so he remained seated for most of the ceremony.

"Thank you, Lord Nadasdy. These last few days, with the thousands of men cheering me on, certainly emboldened me." Smith noticed Ferenc's obvious discomfort while they spoke. "How is your health, my Lord?"

"This is perhaps my last battle, Captain. My legs are causing me too much grief," Ferenc said.

"You have been a great influence on me, my Lord. Your wise words and honourable behaviour will never be forgotten," Smith said.

The two shook hands again, as the celebration continued into the night.

—William Mowat—

Chapter 14 - The Tutor Arrives

The ten-day journey, from Prague to the far reaches of Hungary, had been long and tiresome. The Dowlings had travelled miles of rocky, dirt roads and stayed in various small villages and inns. They had changed drivers and carriages a few times along the way, and now they were on the final approach to Castle Cachtice in the foggy Carpathian Mountains.

As they neared the castle, the faint howls of a wolf pack echoed through the morning fog. The pack seemed playful and satisfied, likely after a massive midnight feast on discarded human bodies beyond the castle wall. Peter and Margaret and their wooden carriage climbed the rugged mountain path, then crossed the heavy drawbridge, stepping into the cold embrace of the ancient stone fortress.

Both Peter and Margaret couldn't help but feel nervous and somewhat fearful, as the castle was ominous and quiet. The mountain air was cool and smelled faintly of animal decomposition, which Peter recognized immediately.

The wooden coach came to a squeaky halt; the driver hopped down to open the doors and then began to remove their luggage.

"Castle Cachtice, my Lord," the driver said to Peter.

"This place is massive," Margaret said.

"I haven't been here for a long time," the driver said. "A lot of rumours swirling about."

"What sort of rumours, may I ask?" Peter asked.

"You smell that?" the driver said, sniffing the air.

"Yes, animal decomposition," Peter said. "Likely a dead deer or horse nearby."

"That ain't no horse," the driver said, unloading the last piece of luggage. "Be careful around these mountains, my Lord. A lot of missing people, kidnapped by ghouls, methinks."

"We will do our best," Peter said. "Plus, I have God on my side."

"Take care, Mr. Dowling," the driver said, tipping his cap. "Miss Dowling."

"Take care," Margaret said. "Thank you kindly," she said, looking at the grandeur of Castle Cachtice.

The driver and carriage exited the castle and went back down the rocky mountain. Peter waved goodbye, but the driver seemed to hurry and did not look back or acknowledge him. Peter then turned to face the castle with his daughter and caught sight of Dorka, Illona, Helena, and Fitzko emerging from the main entrance. Their dark, auspicious sight immediately sent chills through the spines of Margaret and Peter.

"Welcome to the Bathory estate at Castle Cachtice," Illona said. "We have been awaiting your arrival."

"Thank you, most truly. I am Peter Dowling, and this is my daughter, Margaret."

"Lovely," Helena said.

"Let me help you with your bags," Fitzko said.

Margaret looked at the short, gnarled-faced dwarf with a look of curiosity and bewilderment. "Thank you, my Lord," Margaret said.

"Fitzko is my name, and these are Helena, Illona, and Dorka. We are Elizabeth and Ferenc's main servants here at Castle Cachtice. If you have any questions or problems, come to us and we shall answer or resolve anything you need," Fitzko said.

"It is a pleasure to be here and have such a warm welcome. We both have been looking forward to working here with the Countess Bathory and her pupils," Peter said.

"Please do your best not to trouble the Countess, as she is very busy with all the ongoing duties and operations surrounding her estates," Dorka said. She administers many castles, villages, and industries in the area. She is in control of providing for them all."

"Completely understood," Peter said. "King Rudolph II sent me this letter indicating my assignment details and qualifications."

"Excellent," Dorka said. "We will deal with the details later. Please, come inside."

"How was your journey?" Illona asked.

"Quite long, with all the garish mountains and unpleasant passages en route, your Grace. But luckily, I had terrific company from Prague," Peter said, smiling at Margaret.

Peter and Margaret followed the servants inside the cool, dark castle. As they strolled through the front doors, Elizabeth Bathory stood waiting in her evening attire.

"Mister Peter Dowling and his daughter Margaret, your Grace," Fitzko presented.

"Mister Dowling, I'm so glad to see that you have arrived safely. It's a terribly long ride from Prague; the two of you must be utterly exhausted," Elizabeth said in a welcoming tone.

"Quite long, your Grace; but my daughter's presence made the trip a joy," Peter said. "It is an absolute honour to meet you, Lady Bathory. I am humbled and delighted to lend my services to such esteemed nobility."

"This must be Margaret. Aren't you delightful?" Elizabeth said to Margaret. "How are you, my dear? You are courageous to come all this way from England."

"Tired and famished, your Grace, but otherwise delighted that we have reached our destination," Margaret answered.

"Bona sperantibus," Elizabeth said.

"Good things *do* come to those who wait," Margaret responded.

"Intelligent, beautiful, and charming, what a lovely combination," Elizabeth said to Peter.

"Margaret is my most eager student, my lady. She is quite proficient with Greek, Latin, and mathematics and will be a terrific assistant by my side, as we strive to teach and tutor your pupils," Peter said.

Elizabeth was impressed. "Póson chronón eíste?"

"I turned sixteen a month ago, my lady."

"Écheis páei Elláda?" Elizabeth asked.

"I have not been to Greece, my Lady, though I certainly hope to visit sometime in the not-too-distant future," Margaret answered.

"Your youthful eyes are open with vivacity, just like my little son, Paul. The two of you shall get along quite comfortably, my dear."

"I'm looking forward to meeting him, your Grace," Margaret responded.

"I, too, am looking forward to the occasion, your Highness," Peter followed.

"Would the two of you like to join me for dinner?" Elizabeth asked cordially. "There is so much I would like to hear about yourselves and merry England."

"We would be most honoured," Peter answered. "Will Count Nadasdy be joining us this evening?" Peter asked.

"Emperor Rudolph has stationed him at the Castle Sarvar for the time being, and he has recently travelled into Moldova to battle the Crimean Tatars and Ottoman Turks. My dear husband, unfortunately, does not know the approximate time of his return, but I am certain it will be quite some time."

"War is an unpredictable career, your Gracefulness," Peter said.

"It is not just his career; it's his livelihood and his obsession. He thinks only of how to kill, conquer, and dominate his enemy," Elizabeth said.

"All men, though, somewhere in their soul, do hold a love for their family, especially for a devoted wife as beautiful as yourself," Peter said.

"My dear Ferenc is an exception to that rule, Mr. Dowling. This long Turkish war has carried on for too long, and Matthias, Rudolph's brother, is looking to usurp his kin and put a swift end to the carnage," Elizabeth said. "Oh, how I wish my dear Ferenc would return home."

"You must have beautiful views throughout your castle, my Lady. It seems we travelled through the clouds to arrive here," Margaret said.

"The sunrises and sunsets over the mountains are something to behold," Elizabeth answered. "Ferenc gave me this castle as a wedding present, and I have been delighted ever since. Have you been shown to your quarters yet? We picked out a special room for you, my dear."

"No, my Lady, we have not," Margaret said with a smile.

"I have arranged for you to have separate rooms," Elizabeth said to Margaret. "I know how youth enjoy their privacy. Margaret, you will quite enjoy your view. It backs onto our very civil gardens, which are Anglo-inspired, of course, and Peter, your view is just as pleasant. Fitzko will show you to your rooms. I will have dinner at 6:00 pm sharp. I am sure you have plenty of unpacking to do figuratively and literally." Elizabeth turned to leave and spun back around. "Oh, and tomorrow morning, you both shall accompany me to church in the village of Cachtice. There will be a large crowd to celebrate St. George's Day. Pastor Istivan is a wonderful pastor and leader of the faithful."

"That sounds terrific, my Lady," Peter said.

"Fitzko, if you please," Elizabeth said, nodding at her servant.

Peter and Margaret followed Fitzko up the long, winding stone steps to their private quarters. They both smiled at each other at the royal accommodations.

"It already feels like home!" Margaret said.

Atop the first flight of stairs, they made their way down a long corridor and up another small flight of stairs. The hallway was dark, with light only coming from a few candle holders on the wall. Tapestry hung from the ceilings and along the walls, displaying the crests and families of the Bathory and Nadasdy lineage.

Margaret had never been inside a living castle, only seeing those that started deteriorating in northern England and Scotland. Everything was immaculate. Not a cobweb or dust ball anywhere.

"This place sure is clean," Margaret said.

"The Countess takes great pride in keeping things orderly," Fitzko said, "For your own sake, always obey the rules. Keep things clean. Do not upset the Countess, always do what you are told, and you will fit right in."

"As a grammar teacher, I live by rules," Peter joked.

"Ah, here are your rooms," Fitzko said, without laughing at Peter's joke.

They entered the first room with a view overlooking the mountains to the north. The second room, across the hall, had a view south that looked down upon the road leading into the castle.

Margaret chose the first room and ran up to the windows. "This is marvellous!" she said. "I've never felt so royal in all my life!"

Peter could only smile as he and his daughter had finally arrived at their destination. Months of travelling the seas, the mountains, and the landscapes of Eastern Europe were finally over. His feet felt relieved to be on solid ground, his heart was full of momentous joy, and his pockets were full of money for the first time in his life. Peter thought about Margaret's mother and how proud and delighted she would have been to see where they were and how far they had come together.

—William Mowat—

Chapter 15 - St. George's Songbird

A year had passed since the Village of Cachtice last celebrated St. George. Early Sunday morning in the village of Cachtice, a few miles from Elizabeth's castle, the Kovacs family worked hard inside and outside their small home to prepare for church. Jan and his small son Sam had killed a wild turkey and were plucking its feathers. Inside, Catharine and her daughter Maria sat stitching a dress for the upcoming sermon.

"It's not nonsense," Maria pleaded. "Remember, Emily? The last time anyone saw her, she was seen with that deformed hunchback of Elizabeth's. She told me the Countess would arrange her marriage with a royal prince."

"Enough! Elizabeth is our royal guard, our protector and Countess," Catharine said, pulling the thread through the seam.

"She kills women, mother. She cuts off the fingers and toes of her victims. She bathes in the blood of girls."

"Hush now, Maria! I'm about to torture you if you do not keep that trap of yours shut," Catharine said with a firm but light tone.

"She puts pieces of oil-soaked paper between girls' toes, lights them on fire, and watches with amusement. What kind of sick mind would do such a thing? Especially to those that keep their kingdom rich and producing?"

"Enough of this foolish town babble! Finish the dress, then brush your hair," the upset mother snapped.

"Yes, mother."

Jan came through the door and washed the blood and feathers from his hands. "We are going to eat like royalty tonight!" he said, smiling.

"Lovely," Catharine added.

The Kovacs family washed themselves and dressed in their best attire. They eventually made their way to the church in Cachtice for another St. George's Day celebration with Pastor Istivan.

Michael stood waiting patiently outside the church. He caught sight of the Kovacs family walking up the muddy road and beamed with anticipation. Maria wore the lavender dress that she had worked on for a month. Her beautiful sight almost knocked Michael over.

"Hello, Michael," a stern Jan said. "What are you staring at?"

"Hello, Mr. and Mrs. Kovacs," the smiling, nervous Michael said. "I was just admiring how beautiful your family is, sir."

"Lovely to see you, Michael," Maria said, blushing.

"There are nobles from all around Hungary inside," Michael said, pointing to the church. "They've travelled from far and wide."

"We should get inside and find ourselves a seat," Jan said, guiding his family inside.

"Good luck, Maria," Michael said.

The Kovacs family went inside the church. As Michael was about to follow them inside, he saw Elizabeth Bathory's carriage coming from the mountain road. She had four mounted knights riding in front of the lavash wagon. It stopped in front of the church, and out stepped the royal Countess, as regal and distinguished as she possibly could be.

Michael had not seen the Countess in years and only heard rumours about the ongoings. She was a mythical creature, terrifying, mystifying, and utterly alien to his eyes.

Peter and Margaret Dowling then stepped out of the carriage behind the Countess. Margaret looked at Michael and smiled at the stranger.

Michael did not recognize the newcomers but cordially smiled back as he slowly slipped inside the church to await the beginning of the St. George's Day ceremony.

Peter and Margaret admired their surroundings. "What a quaint, well-kept little village," Peter said to his daughter.

"Its architecture and cleanliness are indicative of the Lords and Ladies of the land," Elizabeth said with a smile.

"The church is marvellous," Peter added, looking up to the steeple.

Illona, Helena, and Dorka were the last to emerge from the carriage.

"How does the red brocade and Venetian lace embroidery look?" Elizabeth asked her servants.

"They look perfect," Illona answered.

"Your beauty will be quite admired," Dorka added.

"The most beautiful things in the world are often the most useless," Elizabeth said, "the peacock, for example."

"Point well taken, my lady," Dorka humbly responded.

"Or even the tulip. Without grace, beauty is an unabated hook," Elizabeth continued.

"Yes, my lady," Dorka said.

"There is a young peasant who sings here at church, who is absolutely delightful," the Countess said to Peter. "She transports her listeners to heaven itself."

"I look forward to the music and the sermon, my Lady," Peter said with a slight bow.

As the ceremony was about to begin inside the church, Maria sat at the grand organ, while Pastor Istivan stood at the podium watching everyone enter and take their seats.

"Dear brothers and sisters in Christ, today, we celebrate another feast of St. George, a man whose name has become synonymous with bravery, faith, and the triumph of good over evil. St. George is remembered as a valiant soldier and a martyr who stood firm in his commitment to Christ, even in the face of death. His story inspires us to remain steadfast in our faith, even when Christ calls upon us to make great sacrifices." Pastor Istivan began his sermon and carefully scanned the crowd.

More nobles were attending today, primarily because it was St. George's day, but word had spread throughout the lands that Lady Bathory would attend, so the church was packed.

As Pastor Istivan saw the Countess Bathory and her company arrive and sit near the back of the church, he gripped the pulpit even tighter.

"St. George was born around 280 AD in Turkey. He was a soldier, a man of courage, and a faithful servant of God. As a Christian in a time of great persecution under the Roman Emperor Diocletian, St. George was asked to renounce his faith and sacrifice to the pagan gods. However, he refused to do so. His conviction in the love of Christ was unwavering, and he boldly professed his belief, even though it led to his barbaric torture and eventual martyrdom."

Peter and Margaret had never attended a church sermon with so many people and genuine interest. The Baptists and

Catholics were at odds with each other in England, and people had genuinely grown tired of the back and forth, especially in a time of renaissance and new realization. The once unchallenged belief that Earth was the centre of the universe was crumbling under the weight of discoveries. Astronomy, led by figures like Copernicus and Galileo, revealed a vast cosmos, stirring a revolution in science and how humanity perceived its place in the grand scheme of existence.

For many, including Peter and Margaret, this period marked a moment of awakening, where faith, reason, and inquiry intersected. Sermons were no longer just about enforcing dogma; they would need to evolve and become battlegrounds and meeting places for ideas about identity, the universe, and the very nature of truth.

"St. George was executed, but he did not die in vain. His courage and faith became a beacon of hope for all Christians who would follow after him. His life reminds us of what it means to be a true disciple. Like many saints, his greatest strength came not from his physical power but from his spiritual resolve. St. George's courage wasn't in slaying dragons or defeating enemies with a sword, but in his unshakable faith and willingness to suffer for truth and justice. George's purpose was to relay the universal message that faith is undying."

Illona, Dorka, and Helena scanned the church and realized the number of people who sat looking in the Countess' direction. The servants knew she was noble and intoxicating, but most people looked on with fear and indignation.

"We see St. George slaying a dragon, a symbol of the triumph of good over evil, much like Christ's victory over sin and death. This image resonates with us because we often face insurmountable temptations, struggles, and trials, much like a battle with a dragon," Pastor Istivan said while looking at Elizabeth. "But just as St. George overcame the dragon through his faith in God, we too are called to face our own challenges with the same courage, relying not on our own strength but on the strength that comes from God."

"You see, Margaret," Peter said, "St. George is revered worldwide."

"Let us pray," Pastor Istivan said. "O God, who gave Saint George to your Church as a model of courage and faith, grant that we may follow his example of steadfastness in faith and service to you. May his witness inspire us to live more boldly as Christians, and may we have the strength to face all life's challenges with the conviction of your love. Through Christ our Lord. Amen."

Everyone raised their heads.

Maria Kovacs steps forward as Pastor Istivan introduces her. She sits at the organ, places her hands on the keys, and begins to play. Her voice rises to meet the melody, singing lyrics she has chosen to share for today's service.

Saint George, the martyr, valiant and true,
Thy noble deeds we now do renew.
Thy courage and faith, so bold and bright,
Shine forth as a beacon in the darkest night.

O Saint George, O glorious knight,
Who didst conquer in holy fight,
By thy sword and by thy grace,
Give us strength in this dark place.

Thy valour, so great, did pierce the skies,
Thy shield of faith did God provide.

Thou fought the dragon with steadfast heart,
Now, in heaven, thou play'st thy part.

The congregation was taken in by Maria's flawless, tranquil performance, especially the Countess, who seemed fascinated and enraptured by the hymn.

"St. George's life calls us to be courageous in a world that tells us to be silent about our beliefs. Are we willing to face ridicule, rejection, or even persecution for the sake of God? As a soldier, he was dedicated to protecting the innocent and fighting for justice. His commitment to helping others, even at great personal cost, is a model for us all. The dragon of death has been defeated, and we are granted eternal life through Christ's death and resurrection. Let us pray," Pastor Istivan said, as the congregation all recited the Lord's prayer:

Our Father which art in heaven,
Hallowed be thy name.
Thy kingdom come.
Thy will be done on earth, as it is in heaven.
Give us this day our daily bread.
And forgive us our debts, as we forgive our debtors.
And lead us not into temptation, but deliver us from evil.
Amen.

The Pastor gripped the podium tightly. His head hung low, and to the congregation, he appeared distressed. His restless motion and head-shaking were out of the ordinary, and the mass seemed confused by his strange actions and silence.

Finally, Istivan spoke: "Brothers, sisters, for me to remain at the pulpit, I must disclose something of the utmost importance to you now," the concerned Pastor said.

Elizabeth locked eyes with Pastor Istivan.

As preachers, we hear many complaints," said the Pastor, fixing his gaze on the Countess. "But your Grace has escaped reproach, until now. I can no longer remain silent. I have seen the bodies buried at Castle Cachtice and seen the numerous burns, cuts, and bruises, and most recently, a dog at the castle carrying a human arm. Girls are dying, not because of plague or disease, but because they are being tortured and killed by the Countess of these lands." The Pastor slammed the pulpit. "We need only exhume the bodies to prove me true. You will find the marks and cuts that prove how death occurred! God shall have his vengeance!"

Elizabeth burned with rage. She leapt to her feet. "See here, Minister Istivan!" the Countess shouted. "You will pay for this insult. My husband and I have powerful relatives who will not tolerate your attempt to disgrace me and denounce my name. You have dragged me into a scandal, even placing my husband under public indictment!"

Dorka, Illona, and Helena rose alongside Elizabeth, urging the Countess toward the church's exit.

"I will write to my husband!" Elizabeth screamed.

"If your Grace has relatives, I also have a relative; the Lord God! But for better proof of what I say, let us dig up the bodies, and then we shall all see what you have done!" the Pastor yelled back.

Peter and Margaret, at a loss as to what was happening, quickly rose to their feet, following Elizabeth and her attendants out the door.

Chapter 16 - Rothenthrum

Captain John Smith, Lord Ferenc Nadasdy, and the Earl of Meldritch, at the head of 30,000 eager, battle-hardened men, marched through the mountains into Wallachia, yet another battleground between the Holy Roman Empire and Sultan Mehmed III of the Ottoman Empire. The men had seen war and death on a grand scale.

The Sultan, Mehmed III, at the time of his ascension to the throne, had ordered all of his nineteen brothers to be executed. One by one, they were strangled by his royal executioners. Mehmed, 28 at the time, hired executioners who were deaf, mute, or imbeciles to ensure they were loyal to him and his kingdom.

Captain John Smith, though only in his early twenties, had seen enough bloodshed to last a lifetime. Day after day, battlefield after battlefield, it was still hard to fathom the sheer number of soldiers dying daily.

Meldritch's army had encountered little skirmishes and engagements on its way to Rothenthrum, a Turkish mountain stronghold. His messenger returned on horseback bearing news.

"My Lord, my Lord," the messenger said, bringing his horse to a halt.

"40,000 Tatars have just joined the Turks at Rothenthrum, my Lord," the messenger said.

"Thank you, kind sir. Please relay your message to our captains," Meldritch said.

"Aye, my Lord," he said, riding away.

"What do you think, Captain Smith?" Meldritch asked.

"I think you are not a man of hesitation, my Lord," Smith responded.

"Beyond this pass, we shall take the town and set up for defence of the city," Meldritch said.

"It may be advantageous to attack at night, where surprise is our virtue," Smith said. "I have just the concoction of black powder to lead the way."

"My 'Master of Stratagem' is at it again," said the Earl. "Yet another bold advance proposal that gives us easement in our hour of difficulty. I think Dame Fortune dances are in close attendance on thee."

Meldritch's army marched on the unsuspecting and unguarded town of Rothenthrum and took it without significant incident. The Christian military then prepared for the oncoming 80,000 Muslim enemies. As the sun fell, Smith revealed his scheme and immediately received the consent of the Earl: "This powder-magician of ours would rout the forces of Pluto and distract his realm with horrible explosions of fire. Take what men you need and make what arrangements your judgment prompts, Captain Smith. Tonight, the van is under your command," the Earl said.

Captain Smith relayed the plan to the army commanders, and preparations began. Under the cloak of darkness, Captain Smith, leader of the vanguard, rode towards the enemy with 300 hand-picked horsemen. Each man carried a long spear with fireworks attached to it, designed to make as much noise and light as possible.

The Tatars and Turks were initially fascinated by the sight, but panic set in as the horses got closer. Flashes of light and gunshots all around the Ottoman lines, as things slipped into chaos.

Captain Smith laughed at the effectiveness of his plan. Panic was throughout the Turkish ranks. Soldiers were tripping over one another, men were screaming at the devilish sights, and disorderly retreats were everywhere. Smith's horsemen ploughed into the ranks, spearing and chopping off limbs as they rode.

Ferenc Nadasdy followed with the main body, slaying Tatars and Turks, left and right. The first pass was a remarkable success, but Meldritch had noticed his army was vastly outnumbered, and it was still dark outside. He knew his soldiers might get confused amongst the fighting and have trouble finding their way back.

The fighting continued for hours, thousands lay dead as the sun peeked its head over the mountains. The light revealed 40,000 waiting men in reserve for the Turkish and Crimean army. Soon after sunrise, the 40,000 men charged down the valley toward the exhausted, dwindling Christian army on the blood-soaked battlefield.

"Retreat to the base of the mountain!" Meldritch yelled.

Captain Smith and Lord Nadasdy heard the plans and motioned to regroup at the base of the nearby mountain to mount a proper defence. They fought off the Ottoman army along the way and were able to set up a reasonable defence at the bottom of the mountain.

Ferenc was exhausted, and his legs were writhing in pain. "I don't know how we come out of this!" Ferenc yelled to the regrouping men. "But, I do know there will be a trail of dead Turks and miles of bloody shields and swords!"

Meldritch's army of 10,000 men was hopeless. The sheer numbers of Turks brought fear into his once-hardened ranks. In the Valley of Veristhorne, a few miles from Rothenthrum, the Christian army was being surrounded by tens of thousands of fresh Ottoman troops.

"Captain Smith, I hope you are ready for our final charge!" Meldritch yelled.

Their enemy surrounded Meldritch's entire force. The remaining troops did their best to build barricades and dig in for the last stand. Drums and trumpets from the Turks and Tatars sounded the final push upon the Christians.

Smith was exhausted from the hours on the battlefield, yet his youth instilled a reserve of energy. Far from England, in a foreign land, he still imagined, though desperately outnumbered, he would still come out victorious.

Ottoman cannons began to open up on Captain Smith's position and the rest of the Christian army. Meldritch signalled the charge, and Captain Smith rode onto the battlefield with a hundred other riders. It was brave, yet hopeless, as the Turkish soldiers cut the charge to pieces.

Smith's horse was speared through the ribcage, and he was sent flying to the ground. He landed in a shoulder roll, but the impact dislocated his shoulder from his rotator cuff. He barely made it to his feet as he looked around him at the carnage, and he clutched his left arm. A group of Tatars surrounded the helpless Smith as he painfully drew his sword from his sheath.

From the mountain's base, the Earl of Meldritch, Ferenc Nadasdy, and a handful of nobles retreated through a ravine away from the battle. They successfully slipped away from the battlefield without being injured or captured. However, they left Captain John Smith and the rest of their Christian army to be slaughtered by the overwhelming enemy.

Smith clashed swords with the Tatars. He put up a valiant fight, injuring several soldiers. At long last, after ferocious fighting, Smith was sliced through the back and his right arm. His sword fell to the ground, and eventually Smith fell to his knees. He could feel the warm blood trickling down his back as both arms writhed in pain. Feeling lightheaded, he fell face-first in the mud.

Noticing his regal armour, the Turks grabbed the weary Captain from the ground and dragged him back to their commander.

"My Lord, we have captured one of the Christian Captains," the Turkish soldier said, addressing his commander.

"This man certainly proved himself on the battlefield. His skills were on full display. Look at his uniform; he must be nobility and worth something. Clap him in irons and bring him to the rear," the Turkish Commander said.

"Hardwick! Bishop! Davison!" Smith yelled. "Williams!"

"They're all gone," one of the Turkish soldiers replied.

The physically and emotionally drained Smith was hauled to the rear of the Turkish army in handcuffs. His wounds untreated, he would be transported through treacherous terrain to the Ottoman stronghold in Turkey and sold to the highest bidder at the slave market in Axopolis. As he was dragged away, he watched the last of the Christians die in a desperate last stand. The sun eventually set upon 30,000 dead and dying soldiers and friends in the Valley of Veristhorne.

Chapter 17 - The Red Veil

The Dowlings had been in Hungary for nearly a year and had established a solid routine within the castle. They awoke and had breakfast together, then parted ways shortly thereafter. Peter would begin tutoring, and Margaret would attend a seamstressing session with Illona, Bathory's trusted servant.

Margaret was careful not to say much of anything in the mornings, as rumours were rampant, and she had seen several girls around her go missing. She worked diligently, day after day, with Illona, who was very impressed by her careful stitching and attention to detail.

After a short afternoon break, Margaret would rejoin her father in the grand library, where Peter tutored Paul and a few others in English. Peter also did his best to avoid unnecessary conversation outside his job, especially when working closely with Prince Bathory.

Peter admired Paul. He was a quiet boy, said very little, and worked hard to accomplish the tasks given to him by Peter. Though six years old, he was a fast learner and treated his studies very seriously. Peter had been tutoring Paul in Latin and Greek, two essential languages in the lands of the Holy Roman Empire. The Catholic church was the only religious practice in the Eastern Empire. However, Protestantism had gathered momentum since Queen Elizabeth had re-established the Church of England's independence from the Catholic Church and permanently shaped its doctrine and liturgy through the Elizabethan Religious Settlement of 1559.

Peter and Margaret sat in the library at a large oak desk, reviewing Margaret's essay that she had written over the past month. Young Paul sat by the fireplace, reading a book that Peter had assigned.

Dorka came into the library carrying a scroll. "Mr. Dowling, a letter from London," she said as she handed him the letter.

"Thank you, Dorka," Peter responded.

Dorka turned and exited the library as Peter broke the wax seal and began reading the letter.

"Who is it from, Father?" Margaret asked.

Peter was reading the letter intently. Eventually, he put down the letter and looked up to Margaret. "It's from Ms. Quickly at the Crown and Pheasant. I sent her a letter a few months back, and she has responded." Peter read a few lines. "She sends her best. The Crown and Pheasant business is booming. He continued to read, "And, it appears our good Queen Elizabeth has died without an heir and the new monarch is the son of Mary, Queen of Scots." Peter could only stare at the letter.

"What does this mean? Wasn't Mary found guilty of plotting to assassinate Elizabeth and beheaded for her scheme?" Margaret asked.

"Yes, and her only remaining son, James, has taken the throne and united the Crowns of Scotland and England," Peter replied.

"Why would they allow this?" Margaret followed.

"Robert Cecil is the reason. The man had groomed the entire court for his succession. The country has been waiting for a change, and James already has successors in waiting."

Though it seemed like a peaceful transition, James VI, now James I of England, was baptized a Catholic. Peter feared the already tense situation in England. He genuinely feared there might be a Catholic uprising in England should King James choose to administer Catholicism again in England.

For years, Catholicism had been criminalized since Elizabeth had passed laws that persecuted Catholics. Priests were considered outlaws, fines were administered, and mass was banned throughout the country. Those who sheltered priests were considered treasonous, torture was used to renounce the Catholic faith, hundreds were executed, and even more were exiled to France and beyond.

The people of England, most of whom were in abject poverty, were tired of the Catholic church and its influence over the people. Most resented paying taxes to support the church of far-off Rome, while others hated supporting rich, well-dressed priests and their cultish practices. By 1600, people of Renaissance England felt the Pope was more concerned with luxury, political power, and maintaining influence, rather than spiritual guidance or caring for the needy.

In Scotland, Ireland, and Wales, however, Catholicism was still the practicing religion, and the new King James could, perhaps, ease the laws against Catholics, potentially bringing in a new conflict or even a Catholic uprising.

"I just hope the King maintains the peace and order between Protestant and Catholic," Peter said to his daughter.

"It seems so foolish," Margaret said. "Are they not praying to the same God?"

"You are absolutely correct, my dear," Peter said. "Unfortunately, religion is about power and maintaining that power. The church was once a place of belonging and salvation, now religions and the people that control them are more powerful than countries and kingdoms; empires of blood."

At the opposite end of the castle, Elizabeth Bathory wrote letters and calculated various crops needed for the upcoming winter. As she concentrated on the skill needed to write clearly and legibly with quill and ink, a knock at her door infuriated the Countess and tested her nerves.

"Come in," Elizabeth loudly said.

Dorka entered and presented a letter to the Countess. "A letter from Castle Sarvar, my Lady," the servant said.

Elizabeth took the letter. "Thank you, Dorka. That will be all."

Dorka turned and left as Elizabeth opened the letter addressed to 'My Love'. She read the letter with eager curiosity:

My dear Elizabeth,
A terrible sickness has come upon me with little warning. It has confined me to my bed, where I write this letter now. I have requested that I return home to be with you and the children, but the doctors have strictly forbidden my request. The King believes that if the enemy learns of my sickness, it will be to their advantage and to our disadvantage. I have lost feeling in my legs, and terrible pain continues to eat away at my stomach. I do not have many days left, and I know that when you read this letter, I will have lost the battle with my sickness and be in the hands of the good Lord. I have reconciled with Pastor Istivan, and he has shown

good faith to you and our estate. I have asked the Pastor to perform my eulogy when I am buried. I am also in contact with your dear cousin George Thurzo. He is here with me in my final hours and has agreed to watch over you and our children. My dear Elizabeth, I, Ferenc Nadasdy—Bathory, leave my estate and all possessions to you, The Countess Elizabeth Nadasdy—Bathory. I love you with all my heart and shall miss you as I go beyond. Take good care of our children. Bless you forever, my Love.
Yours Eternally,
Ferenc

Elizabeth dropped to the floor and began crying at the loss of her dead husband. Tears of loss slowly became tears of rage as she began to destroy her entire study. She threw books from the shelves and tore art from the walls. She threw her quill and ink against the wall and smashed an ancient Greek vase on a nearby pedestal.

Ferenc had meant the world to her. He had been the steady centre around which her entire existence revolved. With him gone, the foundation of her life was seemingly crumbling. The thought of moving forward without him felt impossible and meaningless. Grief consumed her like a rising storm tide, inching higher with each breath. She desperately searched for anyone to blame as she struggled to catch her breath. Yet no answer came. The silence was as cruel as the loss itself.

Elizabeth's trembling hands clenched at her dress as she tore through the corridors, her pace swift and unyielding. Servants watched her like a force of nature and dared not approach. The castle's stone walls echoed with the sharp tap of her boots. Every servant knew better than to speak when

Countess Elizabeth was in such a state. They pressed themselves against the cold walls, heads bowed, breath held, as she swept past them. None dared intervene.

Elizabeth descended deeper into the castle, far below the gilded halls and sunlit chambers and into the ancient stone heart of the fortress. Once a place of fear and power, the dungeon had now become a refuge for her turmoil. Down there, she would hope to escape from the endless noise of her thoughts.

Down the cold, winding stone steps she descended. The air grew colder the deeper she went, thick with the scent of mildew, rusted chains, and old blood. There, beneath the earth and the weight of grief, four girls sat shackled in iron restraints, each one bound to the wall by wrists rubbed raw.

All four girls were in varying states of suffering, some bruised, some bleeding, yet all were broken in spirit. Once defiant or pleading, their eyes flickered only with fear and resignation. The stone chamber offered no warmth, comfort, or hope.

She approached the first girl, whose lip trembled as she met the countess's gaze. Elizabeth smiled softly and tenderly, yet the tears streamed down her cheeks. The chained girl stood on shaking legs and stared into Elizabeth's eyes, trying to read what fate awaited her. But the Countess's gaze was unreadable; a chaotic blend of grief, desperation, and a hunger for something she couldn't understand.

Elizabeth raised a trembling hand and brushed a strand of the girl's hair away from her face, almost motherly in gesture.

"You remind me of someone," the Countess whispered. "So young and full of life. Before everything turns to ash."

Then, as if awakening from a dream, her expression shifted. "You'll help me forget. Give me your hand," she said.

The young peasant held out her hand. Elizabeth then pulled a dagger from her dress, grabbed the girl by the wrist, and cut the little finger off her hand. The girl screamed as blood shot all over the front of Elizabeth's face and dress.

It seemed to bring joy to Elizabeth as she grabbed the girl's hand again and began biting her fingers off one by one.

The other girls in the chamber began to whimper and cry at the sight of such horrid cruelty, as Elizabeth continued to bite and gnaw at the hand of the teenage girl. Finally, Elizabeth grew tired of the screams and, with one quick motion, slit the throat of the girl. The body collapsed and smacked the stone floor, as blood oozed from the neck and hand.

Elizabeth rubbed the blood into her lips and skin with a twisted sense of satisfaction and accomplishment. She then licked the blade of her dagger, smiled, and turned toward the other three chained girls.

—William Mowat—

Chapter 18 - Charatza

The Earl of Meldritch was able to escape with most of the Hungarian and Christian leadership through an inconspicuous creek bed, although 30,000 soldiers lay dead in the Valley of Veristhorne. The Crimean Tatars and the Ottoman army obliterated the helpless Christian army, and the rumblings of revolution were already beginning in the royal court of Rudolph II.

Ferenc Nadasy, ailing, weak, and clinging to life, was surrounded by a few officers, the Earl of Meldritch, and Elizabeth Bathory's cousin, Count George Thurzo.

"George," Ferenc said weakly, "ensure my body is returned and buried at Cachtice."

"Have no fear, my friend," George responded, "you and your wife will be reunited."

"Take care of my family, George. They will need your protection," Ferenc faintly said.

"Elizabeth and your children will be protected. You can travel in peace, my friend," George replied.

"You have fought bravely for your emperor and for your country. Ferenc, you will not be forgotten," the Earl of Meldritch followed.

Moments later, in the early evening, Ferenc Nadasdy passed away. The Earl of Meldritch and George Thurzo exited the tent, feeling defeated by the loss of the Black Knight of Hungary and the army that had won so many battles.

Captain John Smith had been captured, thousands were dead, and now the most feared soldier in the eastern Empire had died.

"I must return to Prague and try to salvage this campaign," the Earl said to Thurzo.

"I will return Nadasdy's body home. It will be a difficult period for Elizabeth and all of Hungary. I must ensure she is of sound mind to lead in Ferenc's place," Thurzo said.

"Godspeed, my friend," the Earl said.

"And to you," Thurzo responded. "Any word from Captain Smith or rumours of exchange?"

"Likely transported to Turkey," the Earl answered. "We must assume he is dead and gone."

"Another unfortunate loss for our Empire," Thurzo said.

The following morning dawned gray and sullen, the sky veiled in a thick curtain of clouds that hung low over the hills like mourning shrouds. The air was heavy with the scent of damp earth and the distant smoke of funeral pyres. Death had left its mark on the land.

Count Thurzo, ever the solemn sentinel of duty, oversaw the careful transport of Ferenc Nadasdy's lifeless body back to Castle Cachtice. Wrapped in heavy black velvet, adorned only by the family crest, the once-feared warrior, Elizabeth's beloved, was now nothing more than a silent passenger on a creaking wagon drawn by black horses. Thurzo and the soldiers rode silently, their armour dull beneath the cloudy light, as the procession snaked through the Carpathian foothills.

Meanwhile, the Earl of Meldritch, his duty to the Nadasdy estate concluded, departed for the Royal Court in Prague. There, among the gleaming halls and scheming nobles, he would deliver his report to Rudolph II, whose interests in the affairs of his collection were more important than the ongoing wars against the Ottoman Empire. Meldritch rode quickly, his mind already turning toward courtly intrigues and imperial strategies, leaving behind the haunted lands of his army's demise.

And far, far away, over mountain ranges, across rivers and plains, and through cities buzzing with foreign tongues, a different fate was unfolding. Nearly a thousand miles to the southeast, Captain John Smith sat shackled in a stone-walled cell, the iron cuffs digging deep into his wrists. The once-bold English adventurer, who had sailed the oceans and fought alongside Christian armies, now found himself a prisoner of the Ottoman Empire. Both arms in agony, his uniform torn, face bruised, he sat, slowly trying to heal, behind tired eyes.

For weeks, the young Captain Smith had been beaten and flogged by his enslavers in Turkey. He was now being sold as a slave to a noblewoman in Constantinople.

Smith was then transported to a lavish estate in the Constantinople city centre after he had received medical treatment for his various wounds. The Muslim doctor had set his shoulder back in place and stitched his wounds with care, which had surprised the young Smith. He began to realize that the Muslims were not so different from the Christians; they were caring, honourable, and proud, not barbaric and mindless, like he had been told a thousand times.

At the estate of Charatza, a daughter of a wealthy Sultan, Smith was given a small closet to sleep in and various tasks around the estate. Charatza wanted Smith to work in the gardens, attending various agricultural tasks, including pruning, planting, and cleaning, which he welcomed after the torturous weeks of being chained, beaten, and whipped.

Charatza paid good money for Smith, as he was young, handsome, rugged, and robust in appearance. Given Smith's noble background, Charatza felt he was a good investment, should the Pope ever want to repurchase him.

Smith was called to the courtyard within Charatza's estate. He stood waiting, still uncertain of his new surroundings. Charatza emerged from the breezeway with two accompanying guards.

"John Smith, I am glad you are healing well," Charatza said, looking him up and down with sultry eyes. "We have much for you to do here."

"I am ready for your commands," Smith quickly answered, as he was much happier here than in the enslavement of a cruel Tatar.

"I am curious. I have heard you are a Bohemian noble. Is there truth to this?" Charatza asked.

"I am no Bohemian nobleman," Smith answered. "I have no greater distinction than that of an English gentleman, and I was granted captainship only for my horse-training abilities."

"I have heard the story of the three Turks," Charatza said. "I admire this story. It is also very curious that an infidel has so much honour and fortitude."

"All Englishmen are much the same as I," Smith said. "We are loyal, faithful, and full of honour."

"Your bodies' scars certainly tell a long, brutal story. I would like you to tell me stories of your adventures in the future," Charatza said. "You will work in my private garden.

You will work from sunrise to sunset, with one meal a day. You shall only speak until spoken to," she said in a loud, firm voice.

The two Muslim guards looked at each other. Clearly, Charatza spoke loudly and firmly to draw attention away from her excitement and attraction to the new slave. She found his foreign, brutish nature alluring and was curious about his past and time in the west. His reputation had preceded him, and now she wanted to hear the several stories surrounding his famous adventures. Deep down, Charatza was a romantic in search of magic.

Several weeks passed, and Captain Smith had begun to feel comfortable and confident again. His wounds had healed, he had been eating somewhat well, and was being treated fairly, despite some rough days under the supervision of the guards and slavemaster. The slavemaster guarded in between the high walls of the estate and was cruel and abusive to Smith when Charatza was not around.

Smith had recited his stories of piracy, horseback riding, fighting alongside Nadasdy and Meldritch, and encountering the three Turks. Charatza loved the slave's tales of honour and glory. Smith had thought of escaping, but realized the futility of attempting the feat in the middle of Constantinople. He would immediately be recognized, caught, and executed.

So, Smith bided his time. He hoped that someday, Charatza would grant him freedom and help aid his escape to England.

—William Mowat—

Chapter 19 – A Transition of Power

The Earl of Meldritch and the few remaining Hungarian leaders rode through the Carpathian Mountains to Prague to seek counsel with the Holy Roman Emperor, Rudolph II. It had been a rough ride, especially considering the Earl had lost his army and his best Captain.

The Earl was greeted by Rudolph's brother, Archduke Matthias, instead of the Emperor, which shocked Meldritch.

"Good day, Lord Matthias. Where is the Emperor?" Meldritch asked.

"In the dungeon with his team of alchemists," Matthias responded.

Meldritch and his retinue followed Matthias inside the royal halls of the Prague castle. The goal was to discuss the recent Hungarian uprising led by the noble, Stephen Bocskai, in the wake of the recent Ottoman victory. He and his rebellion began ransacking villages, taking neither side of the Muslim or Christian contingency, but solely a Hungarian one. Bocskai was a significant threat to the Habsburg dynasty and must be stopped.

The people of Hungary had grown exhausted by the war between the Ottomans and the Habsburgs. Fields and villages were left scorched, families torn apart, and productivity reached a near standstill. There was little protection from either side, so Bocskai took matters into his own hands and started assembling his authoritative rule. Elizabeth Bathory and her estates, under the protection of the Habsburgs and the Holy Roman Empire, were now threatened because of the growing rebellion.

In the dark depths of the Prague castle, Rudolph sat looking at three busy alchemists smelting various metals atop a massive coal crucible. The last thing on Rudolph's mind was the uprising in Hungary; he was more concerned with his alchemy and multiple experiments.

The room was full of contraptions and inventions being used to persuade the Emperor that they were, in fact, converting iron and copper to gold and silver through a complicated metallurgical gilding process by the Philosopher's Stone. Rudolph believed this magical elixir would make him rich and grant him eternal life. Matthias knew his brother was being swindled, but Rudolph insisted that the experiments continue.

The Earl of Meldritch entered the room and looked at the Emperor with disbelief. Rudolph visibly looked insane. Fixing his gaze on his team of alchemists, his eyes bulged out from his head, he twitched incessantly, and his whole torso rocked back and forth. Meldritch knew the magicians and soothsayers surrounding the Emperor had him right where they wanted him.

"Your Royal Highness," the Earl said.

Rudolph did not drop his gaze from the working alchemists, nor acknowledge the arrival of the Earl and Archduke.

"You see, Meldritch," Matthias said. "He is completely entranced. Incapable of breaking the spell cast upon him by these sorcerers."

"Bocskai is destroying villages and murdering innocent Hungarians," Meldritch pleaded. "He must be stopped. There must be action."

"There will be no action here; only frustration. Come, I must introduce you to someone," Matthias said.

"I will speak with you tomorrow about the ongoing matters in Hungary," Rudolph said dismissively, without raising his head. "Better yet, I will speak with you when something is to be said."

"You see," Matthias said, frustrated by his unassuming brother. "This has been a waste of time. Follow me."

Matthias and Meldritch ascended from the sweltering depths of the basement chamber, their faces sweaty with traces of soot. Not a single glance was spared for them by Rudolph, who remained engrossed in his own brooding silence, as if the weight of their presence was a burden he could ill afford to bear. The air around them still crackled with the heat of molten metal, but an even fiercer tension lingered between the three men.

As they ascended the worn stone steps, the flickering torchlight cast long shadows that seemed to mirror the dark thoughts in Meldritch's mind. Hungary, his homeland, his first love, the cradle of his family's legacy, felt fragile with the growing ruthless rebellion. The rebels' unrelenting aggression gnawed at the borders, threatening to tear the realm apart from within. And looming over them all, like an unstoppable tide, was the relentless advance of the Ottoman forces, their firepower and ruthless ambition casting a dark shroud over every hope Meldritch held dear.

A knot of despair tightened in the Earl's chest. He feared that, like forgotten ruins, the kingdom would fall and his name and heritage would be lost to history.

The two men eventually arrived at the church of St. George, within the royal palace, where Cardinal Melchior Klesl greeted them.

"Good day, gentlemen," the Cardinal said.

"Your Grace," Matthias said. "First off, thank you most graciously for taking the time to meet with us both today. The Earl of Meldritch and I both support Rudolph ceding the crowns of Hungary and Austria, so that we may take action to save our country from the rebellion led by Stephen Bocskai."

"Pleasure to meet your Holiness," Meldritch said.

"The church has convened with several of Rudolph's family members and agreed that it is time for his brother, the Archduke Matthias, to take control," the Cardinal said, getting right to the point. "Though it has been a difficult decision amongst us. We have concluded that your brother Rudolph should remain the Holy Roman Emperor, in name only, to protect the Habsburg reputation."

"If Archduke Matthias controls the Kingdom, we can take immediate action against these insurgents," Meldritch added.

"Rudolph will remain as the Holy Roman Emperor in title only. Most of the royal family agrees that Matthias is more fit and sound to make decisions on behalf of the Kingdom, including military and foreign affairs," Cardinal Klesl said.

The Earl of Meldritch and Archduke Matthias felt a deep sense of relief and even cautious optimism at the Cardinal's words. Klesl's endorsement was more than a gesture of goodwill; it was a powerful signal that the Church, with all its moral authority and influence, was prepared to stand shoulder to shoulder with the state. For centuries, the balance of power in Hungary had rested delicately between the Crown and the church. Now, with both aligned in purpose, the vision of a peaceful, orderly transfer of power no longer seemed like a distant hope but a very real possibility.

No sooner had their meeting with the Cardinal concluded than Meldritch and Matthias took their leave of the grand cathedral. The thick scent of incense still clung to their cloaks as they entered the crisp afternoon air. Though calm, Prague's streets hummed with the quiet tension that always preceded significant change.

Letters would be dispatched immediately to regional governors, noble houses, and military commanders. Couriers would ride hard across the countryside. Each command, signature, and message, a brick in the fragile bridge that might carry Hungary from fragmentation to unity.

Matthias knew time was his greatest enemy. Delay meant giving the Ottomans a wider opening, the rebels a stronger foothold, and the loyalists more reason to doubt. But with the Church's blessing and their resolve hardened by the hour, Meldritch and Matthias moved swiftly, their steps driven by the hope that Hungary might escape destruction.

—William Mowat—

Chapter 20 - A Porcelain Mask

Pastor Istivan led Ferenc Nadasdy's funeral procession to the small cemetery within Castle Cachtice. Although burials inside the castle walls were uncommon, its owner, Ferenc Nadasdy, was granted an exception. Local sculptors carved a special monument to honour his legacy.

Earlier in the month, Pastor Istivan received a letter from Count Nadasdy asking him to forgive his wife, Elizabeth, and the accusations against her. Although Istivan did not fully trust Elizabeth Bathory, he restrained his hostility while she mourned. Determined to show sympathy and avoid confrontation, he sought only to bury Lord Nadasdy and return to his church.

The entire congregation dressed in black, including Elizabeth Bathory, the grieving widow. Empty-eyed and expressionless, she stood beside the grave and casket, drained of emotion. For two days, she had stared into her husband's open coffin, trying to understand what awaited her. Now, consumed by despair and numbness, Elizabeth clung only to what brought her immediate pleasure.

"His grace fought the good fight against the devil, the world, the flesh, and sin," Pastor Istivan began. "He carried out the word of God with forethought and love; happy is he, gone to the Lord's table. He did not spend his leisure time in idleness but used it to read the Bible. He was good, like a father to his subjects. He passed out food and clothing to the poor and supported the youth in their studies. He ate and drank sparingly and never overburdened his heart with excesses. He ate only once on Saturdays and on all days before holidays, and then only sparingly. The more recognized and great he rose in the eyes of his king and country, the more humbly he conducted himself, because any pretensions were far removed from his inner character."

A hush fell over the gathered mourners as Pastor Istivan paused, letting the weight of his words settle into the silence of the sanctuary. Outside, the church bells tolled slowly, solemnly, marking the passing of noble and devout souls. However, the reality is that everyone knew the truth of his savage history, his brutal wife, and the ongoings within the Nadasdy-Bathory estates.

Margaret carefully observed the Countess. The widow shed no tears, showed no emotion, had no trembling lip, and had no reddened eyes- none of the vulnerabilities one might expect from a woman in mourning. Instead, she had an eerie stillness, like a porcelain figure poised on the edge of cracking, but never quite breaking.

Ever keenly observing people and their hidden selves, Margaret felt a chill settle in her chest. She had long prided herself on reading the undercurrents of emotion, but this was different. Something inside the Countess had fractured, not in a dramatic collapse but in a silent, decisive shift. It was as if a wall had gone up within her, separating her from the pain. This change was more than mourning; it was something colder, deeper. A retreat. A quiet refusal to feel. And that, Margaret feared, could prove far more dangerous than sorrow ever was.

"Let us remember Ferenc not only for the titles he bore, or the honours he received, but for the quiet strength of his faith and the gentleness of his deeds," the Pastor subtly disingenuously continued. "May his example be etched upon our hearts, a guide for those who walk in the shadow of his absence. Though his body lies still, the legacy of his virtue shall endure, like a candle that does not flicker in the wind. May the Lord receive him, and may we strive to be worthy of the path he has shown."

Ferenc's casket was lowered into the grave. A few male servants began to cover the grave in soil as Elizabeth, Fitzko, Illona, Dorka, and Helena returned to the castle. Peter Dowling and Margaret remained at the gravesite, with dozens of others in attendance, trying to make sense of their present and future situation. They realized that the Holy Roman Empire was coming apart at the seams. Hungary was in turmoil, the Emperor was a recluse with fits of melancholy, and Bocskai's rebellion was closing in on the many estates of Bathory.

"The Countess seems vacant," Margaret whispered to her father.

"The Earl's army has been destroyed. The countryside is on fire, and Prince Stephen Bocskai is separating him and the rebellion from the royal court. It will not be long before he claims this castle for himself," Peter said.

"It seems like fire is growing inside her," Margaret responded.

"The Countess is volatile and unpredictable right now," Peter said. "We shall be at our best if you understand my meaning."

"I think we should leave this place," Margaret said, looking at her father.

"It's not that easy, my darling. I have entered into a contract with the Holy Royal Court in Prague. Breaking that contract could result in my imprisonment or death. We must remain here until our contracts are fulfilled or we are given leave," Peter answered.

"You heard Pastor Istivan at church, you heard the faint screams. The horrors carried out by the Countess are not imaginary. She is murdering young girls, and the entire country knows," Margaret pleaded. "We need to leave."

"In this country, peasants have no rights, especially foreigners," Peter replied grimly. "We are completely subject to the will of the Countess. The nobles do as they please, without fear of consequence or justice. If they choose to murder, or punish, or torture, there is nothing anyone can do to stop them."

He glanced cautiously over his shoulder, as if the stone walls might be listening. The weight of those words hung heavily between them, a stark reminder of the fragile line they walked. Peter knew all too well the precariousness of their position. So far, he and his daughter had managed to avoid trouble, like shadows slipping past the watchful eyes of the manor. Young Paul Bathory was thriving despite it all; immersed in his studies, mastering new languages and subjects under the tutelage of patient teachers. His mind was a beacon of hope amidst the encroaching darkness.

Yet Peter could not shake the growing unease in his heart. The land was restless; rebellion stirred in outlying villages, and the brutal hand of violence hovered just beyond the horizon. The horrors they feared were not distant tales; they were looming threats, waiting to shatter the fragile peace they had clung to so tightly.

Taking his daughter's hand gently, Peter forced a small, reassuring smile. "Let us wait a few days and see what unfolds, my dear," he said softly. "Patience is our shield for now. We must be watchful but cautious, for the storms that come will test us all."

His words were meant to comfort, but beneath the surface lay a silent prayer that the coming days would bring not ruin but clarity and safety.

—William Mowat—

Chapter 21 - The Threshing Floor

Captain John Smith had been with Charatza, the wealthy Muslim mistress, for weeks until he was called upon by Charatza's father to work at a grain farm outside the city. Charatza's father had caught wind of his daughter's infatuation with Smith, so he quickly and bitterly intervened. He shaved Smith's head, stripped him of his clothes, flogged him, and clasped an iron collar around his neck. Then, he was dragged to a wheat farm, far from Charatza's doting eyes.

Smith was forced to work the threshing floor with a long, heavy club, called a flail, which was foreign to most Turks, but was an extremely efficient tool. Though he was a good worker, the Turkish guards were severely unkind to the young Englishman.

Hour after hour, day after day, Smith beat bundles of wheat that would soon feed the Ottoman soldiers whom he fought against for years before his enslavement. He pondered about merry England, the cool waters of the Thames River, and the luscious, buxom women of the taverns and brothels. Smith was constantly taunted and whipped by the guards at the farm, but he remained optimistic that he would see home again.

Charatza worried about Smith; she paced up and down the halls of her estate, wondering what types of torment he might be going through. She had grown attached to his presence and lively tales of action and adventure. She sent dozens of letters to Smith that he never received. Not considering the consequences of her words and actions, Charatza's incessant inquiries only made things worse for John.

Smith did think about Charatza, as well. He longed for the days with large meals, cool breezes in the courtyard, and their peaceful privacy together. Though he longed for more accommodating times, he honestly thought about belting the guards across the face with his threshing flail. Obviously, he realized that any type of violence toward his captors would result in death.

A few weeks into his torturous farm job, early in the morning, Smith arose in the loft of the barn where he slept from night to night. He climbed down the wooden ladder and splashed water in his face from a nearby bucket. Usually, this was the best part of his day, but this time, the early morning guard arrived as he was crouching over to splash more water onto his face.

"Infidel!" the guard yelled as he gave Smith a lash against his naked back with his leather whip.

Smith groaned. "I'm not an infidel!" he yelled, as the blood rushed to his head.

The young English Captain grabbed the threshing flail leaning against the barn wall, got up and spun around, striking the Turkish guard in the head with all of his might. The burly Turk immediately fell to the ground with blood pouring from his head. Smith took a few additional whacks at the horizontal Turk to ensure he could not get up and chase him or alert the nearby authorities.

Captain Smith breathed heavily, and the action immediately sent Smith's heart racing. He had little time to waste, as the other guards would be at the barn any minute. So, he stripped the Turk of his clothes, put on the disguise, dragged the body into the corner of the barn and covered him up with straw, so he would not immediately be discovered.

Adrenaline surged through Smith's veins as he burst out of the barn, his heart pounding like a war drum in his chest. Sweat streamed down his face, stinging his eyes, but he didn't dare pause to wipe it away as he sprinted to the post where the Turk's horse was tied. With quick, practiced hands, he loosed the reins, mounted in one fluid motion, and kicked hard into the animal's sides.

The startled horse reared slightly before bolting into the open field, hooves thundering across the trampled tall grass. Smith leaned low over the saddle, urging the horse to go faster. He turned westward toward Prague; his path uncertain, but his resolve absolute. Escape was paramount. The Ottomans would respond swiftly; vengeance was a language they understood well.

As the horse settled into a steady gallop and the chilly night air rushed past his face, something unexpected stirred within him. A smile began to spread across his face, genuine and wide. It felt foreign, like a forgotten language remembered after years of silence. It had been months since joy had even brushed against him, but now, in the saddle, with freedom ahead and danger behind, a strange peace took hold. Still, he reminded himself that caution was not weakness but survival. He would keep his elation in check, keep his emotions locked tight beneath the surface. Until he crossed into Muscovy or reached the safer borders of the Polish-Lithuanian Commonwealth, he could trust no one and afford no mistakes. Every mile westward was a gamble, but the stakes were worth it. He was alive, free, and for the first time in what felt like a lifetime, he had hope.

Chapter 22 - A Crimson Purchase

Even though Rudolph II was still the Holy Roman Emperor in title, Archduke Matthias was now King of Austria and Hungary and made all the significant decisions his brother once made.

Rudolph had become more reclusive than ever. He locked himself in the confines of his room, suffering major fits of depression. His mental fortitude had never been so fragile. Rudolph had never married, though he had illegitimate children all over Eastern Europe.

One of Emperor Rudolf's illegitimate sons, Don Julius, was given Krumlov Castle—an immense estate the emperor purchased as his son's future seat for Holy Roman affairs. Ultimately, though, fate had other plans.

Rudolph, confined in his room, received a disturbing letter stating that Don Julius had become romantically involved with the daughter of a barber. Don Julius had invited the young Marketa to live with him, and her parents agreed because of Don Julius' status. The son of Rudolph began showing signs of madness and, one night, violently beat Marketa within an inch of death.

Thinking she was dead and gone, Don Julius tossed her bloody, naked body out of a window to the rocks below, but the lucky young Marketa miraculously survived and recovered from her severe injuries.

After reading the letter, Rudolph began to sob uncontrollably. His entire world was falling apart. He had no wife, no legitimate children to carry on his title, scammers and fraudsters surrounded him, and now his first son had become a deranged attempted murderer. It gave Rudolph more reason to fall deeper into depression.

King Matthias did not care at all for his ailing brother, though he never made his thoughts known to the public. Matthias was a spitting image of his melancholic brother and was now one of the most powerful men in the world. His sister Anna married King Philip II of Spain, and his other sister married King Charles IX of France. The Habsburgs were indeed a family dynasty, and Matthias was looking to restore pride in the eastern reaches of the empire.

King Matthias' first order of business was dealing with the rebellion in Hungary. After re-establishing relations with Hungary and Transylvania, he sought to end the war with the Ottomans and bring peace to the Holy Roman Empire.

The fall day was overcast and gloomy, only a few weeks after the burial of Nadasdy, as Elizabeth Bathory rode with her trusted servants to Prague. It was very unusual for the high-ranking Countess to be out in public so soon after her husband died. It was not unheard of that wives would remain in solitary isolation for a year, mourning the loss of their spouse. But Elizabeth showed no grievance and little sign of mourning her late husband.

The new King Matthias greeted Elizabeth as her wagon arrived in the Holy Court with royal, welcoming bugles.

"Countess Bathory," Matthias said. "Welcome back to Prague."

Elizabeth stepped down from her elaborate carriage with a beaming smile, wrought with nervous energy. Her demeanour caught Matthias off guard, as he expected a sullen, depressed woman, looking for support. Instead, he looked upon an unsure, seemingly neurotic, frail woman.

"Hello, King Matthias," Elizabeth said. "It's so terrific to see you in your new regalia."

"I cannot help but say that it is strange and quite out of the ordinary to see you so soon after your husband's passing, Elizabeth," Matthias said.

"My husband had been suffering for years, so I had time to prepare myself emotionally," Elizabeth said. "Believe me, I am quite stricken by his loss."

Matthias studied the Countess carefully, sensing the hesitation beneath her composed demeanour. Matthias did not fully believe her story as they spoke, yet he found himself oddly grateful for the sharpness with which she had spun such plausible excuses.

"Your husband was a remarkably brave soldier," Matthias softly said, "He gave his life to Hungary with honour and bravery. He fought valiantly for our cause, never once faltering in the face of danger."

The Countess nodded slowly, her eyes vacant and unwavering. "Yes, brave to the last."

Matthias's gaze darkened. "The Earl of Meldritch was especially saddened by his loss. He barely left the soldier's side in his final hours."

A faint, almost imperceptible sigh escaped the Countess's lips. "The Earl admired him greatly. They were like brothers in arms," The Countess responded.

"I too, will miss the Count greatly," Matthias said.

"My Black Knight of Hungary. Such a sad loss. He will be missed by many. I know he is somewhere better," Elizabeth said.

Matthias changed the topic of conversation: "So, what is it that brings you to Prague in your state of mourning?" Matthias inquired.

"I've come to your lavish city to shop," Elizabeth answered.

After her husband's death, Elizabeth suddenly became the sole heir to a vast fortune, several villages, and sprawling estates and castles. Wealth that once had to be shared was now hers alone to command, and with it came an unprecedented freedom. The Countess answered to no one. The mantle of power, heavy yet intoxicating, rested squarely on her shoulders.

Had Elizabeth known someone she truly trusted, someone wise and steady to confide in, she might have remained within the walls of her family estate. She could have taken the time to carefully evaluate her situation, scrutinize the ledgers, prioritize expenditures, and plan her future with prudence. Such calm reflection and grounded occurrence was never her way.

Her restless heart carried her to Prague, the glittering jewel and fashion capital of the eastern empire, a city that pulsed with life, luxury, and endless opportunity. Elizabeth yearned to escape the shadows that clung to her world, to replace grief with the bright allure of ambition and elegance.

Prague's narrow streets teemed with the finest goods from across the known world: silks dyed in every imaginable colour, rare jewels, exquisite perfumes, and intricate accessories that whispered tales of distant and exotic lands.

Dozens of exclusive shops lined the cobbled avenues, each promising the shopper a taste of the extraordinary.

Elizabeth was now a widow, but her name still carried undeniable weight among the city's elite. Her family's legacy opened doors and softened glances; others typically welcomed her with respect and admiration in the most exclusive boutiques and salons. Vendors bowed, eager to earn her patronage, and the city's social circles buzzed with curiosity and cautious intrigue at the formidable widow newly arrived in their midst.

Elizabeth strolled with Dorka, Illona, and Helena through the markets of Prague. Most people looked at Elizabeth and didn't quite know what to think. She was spending money at nearly every vendor. She paid with quiet authority that defined her nobility and status. In one shop, she bought an assortment of lavish dresses that cost a small fortune.

While Elizabeth's extroverted displays of status may have been those of a noble woman, her nerves were firing rapidly inside her. Her heart raced throughout the day, and she often fell short of breath.

Her increasingly erratic behaviour and dark interests were beginning to circulate, even in the capital city of Prague, far from her home in Hungary. She was oblivious to those around her, finding herself all-powerful, extremely wealthy, and able to do whatever she wanted without consequence.

The city did offer her a momentary escape from the grim ongoings at Castle Cachtice, but she still longed for home and the all-powerful, grim comforts she had surrounded herself with. Little did the residents of Prague know that the woman they saw on their streets was descending into a world of terrifying obsession and cruelty.

Elizabeth entered another dress shop searching for a special dress for the peasant girl she had seen at church on St.

George's Day. The little Kovacs girl with the voice of an angel deserved a brand new embroidered dress when she arrived at Castle Cachtice.

"Good afternoon, dressmaker," Elizabeth said.

"Wonderful to have you in the shop today," the dressmaker responded. "How may I serve you today?"

"Dressmaker, I am searching for a gown for a petite teenage girl. One she might wear for the most elegant of occasions," Elizabeth said.

"Please, let me show you a few designs," the dressmaker said, showing Elizabeth to the back of the shop.

The dressmaker showed her several dresses, some light-coloured, some dark. After a few minutes, Elizabeth spotted the right dress.

"There it is!" she exclaimed suddenly, her eyes sparkling with an intensity that bordered on wild delight.

The dress before her was a deep, sumptuous red, an arresting shade that shone like fire under the boutique's chandeliers. The colour unnervingly mirrored the Countess's own unnatural obsession and wayward spirit.

Elizabeth's finger traced the fabric as she spoke: "The embroidery is exquisite. Delicate and intricate, like a whispered secret stitched into the very heart of the silk." She paused; eyes still fixed on the gown. "I'll take this one."

The dressmaker's face lit up with genuine pleasure. "A wonderful choice, my lady. Bold, yet elegant, with just the right touch of mystery."

Elizabeth was spending money at an alarming rate. She had dropped thousands of gold coins on everything from silk to diamonds to perfume to artwork. She had no cares in the world; no fiscal or domestic responsibilities. Even Dorka, Helena, and

Illona had doubts and concerns, but dared not say anything to their master.

After several days spent amidst Prague's luxury and endless temptation, Elizabeth finally embarked on the long journey back to Castle Cachtice with a packed caravan of goods and riches. The grand city's glittering facades faded behind her, replaced by the dense forests and shadowed hills that cloaked the winding roads of Hungary. Despite the many shopping days and travelling, the tempest raged inside Bathory and grew fiercer.

Bathory's thoughts were dark and relentless, swirling like a storm cloud ready to burst. The desires simmering beneath her polished exterior during those costly days in Prague now surged forward with brutal clarity. Urges and cravings that had once been whispered in the quiet corners of her mind now demanded full attention. There was no respite, no mercy. The Dragon, her insatiable, merciless inner force, demanded sacrifices, blood offerings, and domination.

—William Mowat—

Chapter 23 - The Gynaeceum

In the Village of Cachtice, Elizabeth's dwarf servant Fitzko arrived with his wagon to escort Maria Kovacs to the castle. Chosen personally by Bathory to attend her exclusive finishing school within the towering walls of Castle Cachtice, Maria had been singled out for her extraordinary beauty and rare musical talent. It was whispered in the village that her voice could charm nightingales into silence and put raging bulls to sleep. Along with the honour of this selection, Maria was promised a future marriage to a nobleman of considerable standing, though no name had yet been given. But Maria's heart was already spoken for, as it still belonged to Michael, the young Cachtice man with warm eyes and calloused hands.

As she exited her home, clutching a small, carefully packed satchel, Maria's steps were slow and uncertain. The morning light cast long shadows, and the air carried a heavier chill than mere weather. She paused beside Fitzko and the wagon, glancing back one last time. Her mother stood stiffly, arms crossed to hide trembling hands. Her father avoided her gaze, staring instead at the ground. Beside them, little Sam waved with naive excitement, unaware of the undercurrents in the air. Michael had also made it across town to say 'goodbye'.

He stood, face pale, and eyes burning with helplessness. He managed to get a tight smile, raising his hand in a gesture of farewell that looked more like surrender.

Maria forced a smile, though her heart ached. She knew this was more than just a journey to a finishing school. She was stepping into the Countess's world, a world of secrets, shadows, and whispers that turned warm blood cold. With a final breath, she climbed into the wagon, the heavy door closing behind her like the lid of a casket. Jan and Catharine Kovacs did not have a choice in the matter, as the Countess always received what she desired, and she wanted young blood.

"I'll miss you," Maria said, waving goodbye.

"We love you, Maria," Catharine said, as she began to cry.

Fitzko gave a sharp flick of the reins, and the carriage staggered forward, wheels creaking as they rolled over the uneven dirt road. The horses trotted steadily, their hooves clapping against the packed earth as they left the quiet village behind. Maria leaned closer to the small, smudged window, watching as the cluster of thatched rooftops disappeared behind a bend in the path.

As they climbed higher into the foothills, the road narrowed and grew rougher. The air thickened with fog, and the temperature plummeted sharply as a bitter wind howled down from the jagged peaks ahead, rattling the wooden frame of the coach. Maria shivered, pulling her wool shawl tighter, but the chill that ran up her spine had little to do with the cold.

She absently twirled the end of her long brown hair between her fingers, a nervous habit that offered little comfort. Her thoughts wandered to Castle Cachtice looming ahead in the shadows of the Carpathians. What secrets lie behind its high, timeworn walls? What kind of life awaited her there? She had been told she would receive courtly training and learn the art of etiquette, language, and decorum under the guidance of esteemed nobles and tutors. It was, by all accounts, a great opportunity.

But rumours clung to the castle like the fog; whispers of missing village girls, of blood-stained floors and silenced screams. She had heard them all. Superstitious nonsense, she had told herself. The truth, surely, was far less sinister. The plague, poor sanitation, and illness were the real culprits behind the funerals. Still, the unease lingered. Whatever lay ahead, she would face it with resolve. But even as she told herself that, her hand would not stop twisting her hair, and the sense of foreboding refused to loosen its grip.

Finally, Fitzko broke his silence. "The Countess tells me you have a wonderful voice!" he yelled from the front of the carriage.

"Thank you, yes, I've trained my whole life!" she yelled.

"The Countess will treat you well," the simple dwarf said with a sinister smile.

Maria sat back and uneasily smiled at the driver's comment. She hoped her entire experience would be short, smooth, and void of blood or violence.

Inside the massive Castle Cachtice, Peter Dowling and his daughter waited for the new arrival. Peter and Margaret had seen Maria perform on St. George's Day and were excited for her to join the training at Cachtice. Both Peter and Margaret missed the cultural diversity of London and longed for the theatre, music, and performance.

The Dowlings sat in the southwest library of Castle Cachtice. Margaret read a brand-new book, while Peter organized a bookshelf. Week after week, Peter tutored and

Margaret trained. Peter was happy to have more company within the walls, but he had come to the actualization of the gradual disappearance of girls throughout the months. Some might be in the refinement school for months, and for some, it might be days. Peter ensured he never questioned the sudden disappearances but pressed on with his teaching duties.

Margaret was always grateful to have another friend her age join them, but she, like Peter, was worried about the gradual disappearances. She swore she had heard screams from the castle's depths, but her father told her it was the wind, and she was not to worry or mention it again.

The Dowlings' suspicions had swelled in recent weeks. Castle Cachtice was changing dramatically. Elizabeth Bathory, once the radiant and commanding matron of the estate, was becoming increasingly elusive. She rarely attended the public dinners anymore, emerging only late at night or when summoned by matters she deemed urgent. Her temperament had grown unpredictable, flaring without warning.

The abnormal behaviour of the Countess was accelerating and becoming a threat to anyone and everyone around her. Peter had trained his daughter to be one hundred percent obedient and not to speak unless spoken to. The concerned father had several conversations with Margaret, teaching and persuading her to talk without emotion, and to always remain conservative with her voice and opinions. The Countess and her servants were temperamental and easily agitated about most things; even the slightest comment could set them off.

Then there was the matter of young Paul, Elizabeth's youngest son. Without warning, he had been sent away to Prague under the care of a distant cousin. Officially, it was said to be for his education and safety, away from the whispers of rebellion that were beginning to stir in the hills. But many suspected otherwise. It was almost as if the Countess herself feared what was coming, or what she was becoming.

"Father, what is a tergiversation?" Margaret asked as she inspected the page of her book.

"Ah! Great question. It comes from the Latin term 'tergiversari', meaning the avoidance or showing reluctance. We use this term in English to avoid saying a clear-cut statement."

"That makes sense now," Margaret said, looking back at her book.

Peter smiled at his daughter's inquisitiveness and longing for knowledge. As she read, Peter watched and admired her. He was reminded of how much Margaret and her mother were alike: fierce learners, nurturers at heart, and beautiful beyond compare.

Peter looked down and began reading a periodical from London. The last paper he read outlined Queen Elizabeth's death and King James I's succession to the thrones of England, Scotland, and Ireland. At the top of the paper was a picture of the new British flag created to symbolize the unification of Scotland and England under one King. The Union Jack displayed the red cross of St. George and the cross of St. Andrew, the patron saint of Scotland.

The picture of the Union Jack gave Peter a surge of pride and longing for home. He read on and discovered King James' desire to colonize the New World. The King and a few investors helped create the Virginia Company, which had its heart set on the northeast shores of North America.

There was also a short article entitled 'The Capture of Guy Fawkes Under the British Parliament'. Peter was not quite sure what it could have meant. He had never heard the name, nor could he comprehend what he could have been doing under parliament. He read on:

On the night of November 4, 1605, Guy Fawkes, a dispirited Catholic and key conspirator in a plot to kill King James and the entire British parliament, was captured beneath the British Parliament, guarding a pile of wood, close by was enough gunpowder to blow New Westminster into oblivion.

The plot was driven by a group of English Catholics, including Fawkes, who resented the King's anti-Catholic policies and the general persecution of the faith in England. The conspirators planned to ignite 36 barrels of gunpowder hidden in a cellar beneath the House of Lords during the state opening of Parliament. Fawkes has been taken to the Tower of London for further investigation.

"Margaret, read this," Peter said, handing his daughter the periodical.

Margaret read the paper and turned to her father. "They tried to kill the King?"

"Apparently," Peter said. "It didn't take long for a Catholic upheaval."

As Peter and Margaret chatted in the library, Fitzko came through the doors, followed by Maria Kovacs. Maria was timid as she was guided through the castle. Fitzko approached Peter and Margaret with his mischievous smile.

"Mr. Dowling, Miss Dowling, this is Maria Kovacs, a peasant girl from the Village of Cachtice," Fitzko said.

Peter and Margaret both introduced themselves to the young, frightened Maria.

"Maria will be our newest lady in training. She will also serve as entertainment for celebrations," Fitzko said. "She is a gifted musician."

"We heard your performance at Pastor Istivan's mass on St. George's Day. We were quite taken with your voice," Peter said to the young girl.

"Thank you, my Lord," Maria said, barely making eye contact.

"You shall be seeing more of Miss Kovacs, as she will be one of your students, Mr. Dowling," Fitzko said.

"I look forward to the occasion," Peter responded.

Fitzko and Maria stepped out of the castle's grand library, their silhouettes swallowed by the long shadows of the corridor. The heavy wooden doors creaked shut behind them, muffling the soft echo of Maria's reluctant footsteps and the faint shuffle of Fitzko's uneven hobble.

Peter and Margaret recognized the young Maria from St. George's Day and remembered Pastor Istivan's unsettling sermon. Known for his cautious diplomacy, the old priest had shocked the congregation by raising his voice in righteous condemnation of the Countess. He spoke of blood, corruption, and moral rot that had infected the highest halls of power. Though he never named her, everyone in the chapel knew exactly whom he meant. Afterward, villagers from beyond Cachtice came forward with grim stories of daughters gone missing, strange men patrolling the woods near the castle at night, and secret carts wheeled away under the cover of darkness. For the first time, the surrounding villages were beginning to speak openly. They were starting to stand up to the Countess.

The chill in the air deepened as Peter and Margaret knew something terrible was building within the walls of Castle Cachtice, and they had to make a contingency plan.

Chapter 24 - A Holy Plea

Elizabeth Bathory's cousin, Count George Thurzo, had steadily risen to become the most powerful nobleman in the kingdom, second only to the newly crowned King Matthias. A shrewd and pragmatic man, Thurzo welcomed Matthias's ascendancy, grateful that the new monarch had succeeded Emperor Rudolph. Under Matthias's reign, Thurzo saw a chance to stabilize a realm long torn by war and rebellion.

His most recent accomplishment was brokering peace with Stephen Bocskai, the charismatic leader of the Hungarian uprising that had ravaged the countryside for months. Bocskai's rebellion, fueled by grievances over religious oppression and political marginalization, had threatened to plunge the region into chaos. But through delicate diplomacy and tireless negotiation, Thurzo had helped seal a peace treaty that promised to quell the unrest, at least for the time being.

Now, seated at a heavy oak desk in the quiet sanctuary of his study, Thurzo carefully reviewed the budgets for his vast estates. The room was lined with shelves burdened under the weight of dusty ledgers and maps detailing every acre of his sprawling domains. A fire crackled softly in the stone hearth, casting flickering light across the room.

His fingers traced the columns of numbers and accounts, calculating the expenses necessary to keep his lands prosperous and his people secure. After years of turmoil and military campaigns, Thurzo relished the rare opportunity to focus on the mundane yet vital governance tasks: ensuring the peasants were fed, the roads repaired, and the harvests bountiful.

Taking a slow breath, he pushed back from his desk and gazed out of the tall window overlooking the rolling hills of his estate. As he pondered the future and stared down, his servant entered his study.

"My Lord, Pastor Istivan from Cachtice has arrived," the servant said.

"Send him in," Thurzo responded.

"Yes, my Lord," the servant said as he exited the study.

Moments later, Pastor Istivan came through the doors after riding for two days through the mountainous terrain. He had come bearing signatures from various villagers and some from wealthy business owners, regarding the ongoing activities at Castle Cachtice.

"Good evening, your Grace. I am Pastor Istivan from the village of Cachtice. I have come a great distance to meet with you. I hope I am not intruding."

"I have received your letters and am glad you have received my invitation," Thurzo said with a subtle smile.

"Thank you, my Lord. I am glad you have received me," Pastor Istivan responded.

"You have come a great distance, Pastor. What is it that I can do for you?" Thurzo came straight to the point.

"Sir, I have come here with a great concern for the lives of the people in my village," Istivan pleaded.

"What's troubling you, priest?"

"My Lord, it's your cousin, the Countess Bathory."

"Go on," Thurzo said.

"We've had several young women go missing, your Grace. Villagers, peasants, now daughters of shopkeepers, and craftsmen," Istivan said.

"I am aware of this matter, Pastor. You must remember that she is nobility, a class above peasantry. The law protects her in these matters," Thurzo said.

"She commits evil deeds, brutal rituals like the devil himself, your lordship." Istivan was doing his best to convince the Count.

"Pastor, she's of high nobility, untouchable by our country's courts," Thurzo answered.

"Yes, sir, but are you not second only to King Matthias? I have buried dozens of bodies over the past years, and things have been steadily increasing. Your cousin has become a monster since the death of Count Nadasdy and shows no sign of slowing down," Istivan said. "Death after death, funeral after funeral, all closed caskets, no explanations, only vague, unconvincing answers."

"These are dangerous waters, Pastor. Could the deaths not be related to the plague that has run rampant through our country?" Thurzo inquired.

"Always closed caskets, my Lord. Sometimes two, three bodies to a casket. I have never been shown the interior of a single casket. Which tells me the bodies are likely mutilated or disfigured. Only her servants, those demons of Cachtice, know what is inside those caskets. They abide by the book of Shadows, sorcery, your Lordship, this could be prosecuted in court, could it not?"

"Understand my position, Pastor. Countess Bathory is a significant political figure in this country. Unless word is given from King Matthius himself, I stand unable to intrude or invade her castle walls. And even if we could convict her, she could never be punished by death, only by imprisonment," Thurzo explained.

"Your Highness, we need not kill her; we need only to stop her twisted, hellish amusements," Istivan pleaded.

"I will take your evidence to the King, but understand that as of yet, there is nothing that I can further do in this matter," Thurzo said as he stood from his chair. "Continue to collect stories and signatures from victims and their families. Have them record the smallest details and anything pertinent to a potential conviction. Should her behaviours lead to a trial, we will need all the evidence we can gather."

"Thank you for your valuable time, your Grace," Istivan said, as they shook hands.

Pastor Istivan felt pleased with Thurzo's reaction to the missing girls within his village. He gave him first-hand accounts that helped solidify his stance toward his cousin. However, Istivan knew his job was not done. He planned on getting testimonies from everyone, including the members of the Kovacs family. Istivan knew their testimony would be dire, as their daughter was well known, talented, and the next potential victim of the Countess.

Chapter 25 - The Silk Road

After several gruelling days and nights traversing the harsh, unforgiving landscapes beyond the Crimean steppes, Captain John Smith stumbled upon what he had long hoped to find: the fabled Silk Road. Half-starved, his Muslim disguise tattered from brambles and wind, and surviving only on the meagre contents of a corn sack he stole from his Tatar captors, Smith's body ached with exhaustion. Yet as he crested a low ridge and beheld the sprawling, dust-worn trail below, a surge of wonder and relief stirred.

The Silk Road was pulsing with the movement of caravans; long, winding processions of camels, mules, and merchants, their cargo clattering softly beneath the rising sun. He watched silently, awestruck by the sheer diversity of people and goods weaving across this ancient highway.

Every figure he observed represented a thread in the tapestry of a global network older than empires. The Silk Road was not just a trade route but a meeting ground of civilizations, a place where ideas, religions, and stories moved alongside silk, spice, and precious metals. It was a road lined with danger: bandits, disease, and the ever-present threat of political unrest, but it also shimmered with opportunity.

Captain John Smith was ragged and weakened, but his discovery energized him. He might find a path home among these pilgrims, traders, and fortune seekers.

He tightened the remnants of his cloak around his shoulders, took a final bite from the cornmeal he had rationed for days, and descended toward the road.

Smith was careful not to talk to anyone; he disguised himself well and blended in with the other weary travellers. His biggest worry was that someone might discover the galling iron necklace around his neck. It had been around his neck for so long that calluses formed around it. Its discovery would automatically announce that he was an escaped convict, and the authorities would be close behind. So Smith tied a piece of fabric around his cloak, just below the chin, which covered the collar completely.

Smith rode the Silk Road for weeks. Day after day, he eventually reached Muscovite, a welcoming part of the Christian world. The Muscovites filed the bondage necklace and released Captain Smith from his restraints. The necklace had left a nasty, bloody scar, which the village doctor bandaged.

He was able to find a translator within the city, where he was given some money from the local magistrate, who was more than willing, after hearing his tremendous story across the battlelines of Eastern Europe. The magistrate also outlined a direct passage to Transylvania, where the young Captain hoped to meet again with the Earl of Meldritch and re-insert himself into the military ranks.

Smith smiled and thanked the magistrate, as he secured what little belongings he had, mounted his tired Crimean horse, and once more set out towards the Carpathian Mountains, where winter was fast approaching.

Inside Castle Cachtice, Elizabeth's reign of terror continued, as she had become less cautious and secretive about her gruesome torturings inside the damp, stone walls. Screams had awoken servants in the middle of the night, blood trails were becoming more frequent on the floors, and the smells of human decomposition were spreading unsettlingly throughout the castle and beyond.

Throughout the past months, Peter and Margaret devised a secretive escape plan. Things were becoming far too horrific, the sounds, the smells, the behaviour of the Countess, so they decided to plot an escape in the middle of the night and start riding toward Venice, where they might find an English vessel to take them home.

Though both Peter and Margaret wanted to save the other confined girls, they knew it would mean immediate death for treachery and deception. Their actions in the coming weeks would need to be discreet and away from the dozens of prying eyes and ears around the castle.

Margaret and Maria had become especially close after their first few weeks together. They were about the same age and shared stories of England, William Shakespeare, Ben Johnson, religion, music, and relationships. It was difficult for Margaret to keep the escape plan a secret from Maria, as she desperately wanted her to come with them. Maria was talented, funny, and innocent of all evil, but Peter was adamant that only the two of them would plot the escape.

Day after day, night after night, Margaret and Peter planned. They discussed the route they would take, the clothes they would wear, and the items they would need. Margaret began working on a traditional riding dress, and Peter started to map out the best way to Venice, where he and his daughter might find a ride home to England.

The Dowlings realized they would not get anywhere without a horse. Stealing a horse from the Countess would be difficult, as the stables were closely guarded and challenging to get into at night. Margaret meticulously observed and recorded all the movements of the stable masters and guards, and also took some time off to explore and ask questions of the stable master. From her window, she wrote times of shift changes, guard movements, and sleeping habits, and jotted down anything else of use.

Maria Kovacs had become little more than a musical blackbird for Countess Bathory, her delicate fingers coaxing haunting melodies from the strings of her lute, her voice rising and falling in eerie harmony whenever the Countess summoned her. Between performances, Maria was subjected to relentless training in the gynaeceum. She mastered intricate dances, perfected her posture, absorbed the complex rules of etiquette, and honed skills in sewing, reading, and writing, all the skills needed to maintain the facade of a noble lady-in-waiting. Yet, despite the veneer of refinement, Maria's nights were restless and filled with dread. She scarcely slept, haunted by the ever-present stench of decay that seeped through the castle walls.

The sun, eventually, shone through the small window in her quarters. Maria began the day groggy and nauseous, after a terrible night's sleep. She had tossed and turned through nightmares and found herself staring at the ceiling for what seemed like hours at a time. She put her feet on the cold stone floor and began to dress as there was a loud bang on her door.

She rushed and opened the door to Countess Bathory, who looked dishevelled and angry.

"Good morning, Countess," Maria said, bowing.

Elizabeth stared at Maria long and hard.

"Is everything alright, my Lady?" Maria said.

"Everything is not alright," Elizabeth said, finally breaking her silence. "A young lady stole food from my table. Caught this winter's morning."

"That's terrible," Maria responded.

"I would like you to come with me to the courtyard," Elizabeth said. "I expect you downstairs in 10 minutes," the Countess said, spinning around and heading out the door.

"I will be there," Maria said.

The young Maria did not know what to make of the Countess. She was unpredictable and seemingly always on edge, so she dressed as fast as possible, put on a jacket and scarf, and shuffled down the cold steps to find Elizabeth and an entourage of servants waiting by the front door. In the hands of Fitzko was a young peasant girl whom Maria had met a handful of times. Maria shied away from looking the girl in the eyes.

Behind the dozens of servants, Maria noticed Peter Dowling and his daughter Margaret, who looked displeased at what was about to transpire.

The helpless girl was dressed only in a nightgown and was barefoot. Her complexion was grey and blue as she stood shaking.

"Ah, Maria is here," Elizabeth said. "Dorka, Illona, Helena, lead the procession outside."

Dorka and Helena opened the grand oak doors, exposing the frigid winter winds. Everyone moved outside into the courtyard. A semicircle of wooden chairs and a grand, hand-carved chair were set up for the Countess Bathory.

Everyone took their seats, including the Countess, who looked quietly excited by the ordeal. "Good morning, ladies and gentlemen," Elizabeth announced. "This young lady, whom I invited into my house, provided shelter for, nourished unconditionally, both mentally and physically, and embraced as a daughter, has deceived me in my own home."

Maria looked at Peter and Margaret, still unsure what had transpired. Peter and Margaret's heads were both facing down at the ground, as if they could not watch what was about to transpire.

Fitzko emerged from the castle, escorting the frightened girl to the middle of the semicircle of spectators. Following behind Fitzko was another servant carrying two buckets.

"This young Liza has betrayed my heart and soul, and stolen from me, despite my love and trust. We must not forget my generosity, and confuse that with naivety," Elizabeth lectured. "I am glad my most promising students are here today," she said, looking at Margaret and Maria. "The Lord has blessed us with perfect weather for the occasion."

Fitzko sat the frightened Liza down and tied her hands and legs to the wooden armchair. As Elizabeth rose from her chair, Fitzko stepped back. As she approached the girl, Elizabeth pulled a pair of long shearing scissors from her winter jacket. She smiled at Liza as she began to cut away her white nightgown.

Piece by piece, Elizabeth cut and threw the garment to the ground, leaving the poor girl shivering naked in the subzero temperatures.

Peter was horrified by the scene, but knew he could not expose his displeasure, for fear of repercussions on himself or his daughter. They were fast approaching the spring, where they might try to make their escape. The Dowlings knew the slightest clue might spoil their surprise flight.

"The guilty must be punished," said Elizabeth, as she sat down in her exotic chair.

Liza was shaking uncontrollably as Fitzko picked up the first bucket and poured water slowly over the naked girl. Steam rose through the air as the girl screamed and gasped for breath.

Both Margaret and Maria began to cry at the torturous act. Peter gripped his daughter's hand tightly. "Hush now," he said. "We must not make a scene."

Elizabeth, Dorka, Helena, and Illona watched with intrigue and genuine pleasure as Liza slowly drifted from shivering uncontrollably to perfectly still, void of breathing. Her head was bent over, and her hair froze straight down as the steam eventually stopped. Ice crystals began to form all over the girl.

"No fight left?" Elizabeth screamed.

The girl's head suddenly lifted and shocked the onlookers. She looked directly at Elizabeth. "I'm sorry," she whispered, as her head collapsed back down.

Fitzko poured another bucket of water over her head, and a few minutes later, Liza was frozen solid with a layer of ice around her entire naked body.

"What a wonderful sculpture she has made," Elizabeth said. "She put up extraordinarily little fight, though. I thought she would have lasted longer."

Peter, Margaret, and Maria stood frozen in place, their stomachs churning with disgust and horror at both the grotesque scene before them and the chilling words of their hostess.

"Let this be a lesson to anyone who resides within these castle walls," the Countess declared, her voice smooth as silk and twice as cold. A smile curled on her lips, serene, almost amused. "Stealing from my table shall be repaid with death. Liza will remain here, as a statue carved by winter's hand, until the thaw of spring. Every day, she will remind us to honour our masters and respect our generous hosts. We do not steal. We do not lie. We do not disobey."

With that, Countess Bathory turned and strode back into the castle, her velvet-clad servants following in her wake. Maria, Margaret, and Peter hesitated only a moment before trailing after her, the bitter wind biting at their skin. As they passed the lifeless, frozen Liza, her limbs stiff with frost and her eyes wide and glassy, they forced themselves to keep their faces blank. The horror twisted inside them like a knife, but any flicker of sorrow, flick of the eyes, or trembling lips might betray them. And they knew too well what the consequences of sympathy might be in a place like this.

Captain Smith rode through the Carpathian Mountains and began recognizing the surrounding Transylvania. He was glad he was close to familiar grounds, as the biting cold was becoming too much for him and his overworked Crimean horse.

The young Captain rode onto the estate of the Earl of Meldritch and smiled at the memories he had with the Earl on the battlefields of the Long War. He supposed he would have likely been presumed dead on the Rothenthrum battlefield. It was a hellish battle, where thousands were left for dead, as the remnants of the Christian army fled into the mountains.

Finally, after nearly a month of riding from Crimea along the Silk Road, he spotted the lavish home of the Earl. He dismounted his horse and walked the final mile to the doorsteps.

The Earl of Meldritch emerged from his home with a rifle and squinted at the approaching horseman, who appeared to be Turkish, with a fashioned turban and long flowing robes.

"Halt, Muslim rider!" the Earl yelled.

"Fear not, Earl of Meldritch, it is I, Captain John Smith," he yelled.

"Smith! Back from the dead?" the Earl yelled.

"This is true, my Lord. Your master of stratagem has travelled far and wide to reunite with you!" Smith said, smiling.

Eventually, the Earl recognized Smith's red beard and face, smiled and ran down the steps to greet the weary traveller.

"Back from the dead, indeed," Meldritch said. "Where have you been? How did you get here?"

"Well, it is a long story, do you have a minute?" John cheekily said.

"Come in, my dear boy," the Earl said, putting his arm around Smith. "Let us put as much food and wine in our bellies as we can fit!"

The Earl and Smith were reacquainted over the next couple of days, while the young Captain recovered his strength after months of malnutrition and exhaustion. Smith told him his story of slavery, his affair with Charatza, and his escape from the Crimean wheat fields and onto the Silk Road.

The Earl communicated the newly formed peace brokering at Zsitvatorok between the Ottoman Empire and the Holy Roman Empire. He also outlined his dismay that they would no longer be able to fight together again, because of the existing peace. The conflict had finally brought some civility to the area, and Meldritch was glad to have it.

Hungary and Transylvania were granted freedom of religion and the right to elect their own independent princes in the future. Meldritch knew the democratic process worked well in other parts of the world and openly invited the new form of government.

Smith and Meldritch shared a hearty meal of turkey, potatoes and carrots at dinner. The aroma of gravy and freshly baked biscuits made Smith's mouth water, as he showed gratitude for eating anything besides stale corn.

"This turkey tastes especially good, my Lord Meldritch," Smith said, taking a bite. "Corn, corn, and more corn is all I've had this past month."

"Well, I'm glad you're enjoying it and thankful," Meldritch said with a smirk.

"I don't think I will ever eat corn again," Smith joked.

"I don't blame you," the Earl said with a chuckle.

"Any word from Rudolph in Prague?" Smith asked.

"Well, my friend, he still holds the seat of the Holy Roman Emperor, but by name only. His brother Matthias has taken over most forms of government. The brotherly feud is almost at an end, thank God. Rudolph has slipped completely out of touch. Having visited a while back, his eyes bulged out of his head, and his melancholic state left him detached and secluded from any meaningful conversation."

Meldritch moved to his office desk and found a recent letter he had received from King Matthias.

Rudolph had just received more news concerning his son, Don Julius. Despite almost murdering his girlfriend because of his delusional schizophrenia, she was forced to return to his bed, at the estate given to him by his Emperor father.

Meldritch read from a nearby paper:

On the 18th of February, Julius, that awful tyrant and devil, bastard of the Emperor, did an incredibly terrible thing to his bed partner, the daughter of a barber, when he cut off her head and other parts of her body, and people had to put her into her coffin in single pieces.

Rudolph was now confronted with the news that his son was a murdering madman. He did not defend his son and ordered Don Julius's imprisonment for the remainder of his life.

"As you see, Captain Smith, Rudolph is slipping away. King Matthias now holds the power and he is to be commended for his actions," Meldritch said. "King Matthias has also become aware and rather alarmed by the behaviours of Countess Elizabeth Bathory at Castle Cachtice."

"What has been happening at Castle Cachtice?" Smith asked.

"Word from Prague is that she is on the brink of emotional collapse and insanity. For years, hundreds of peasants have gone missing from surrounding villages. Priests have come forward with eye-witness testimonies and letters of implication. These holy men have called on the King to take action against her murderous, wicked wrongdoings," Meldritch answered.

"What has she been doing?" Smith inquired.

"She has been torturing young girls. Those priests have brought their cases and lists of witnesses forward. They spoke of mass burials, sometimes, two or three bodies in one casket. Now, girls from more prominent families have gone missing."

"Sad to hear that Ferenc Nadasdy's legacy has fallen under a cloud of shame," Smith said.

"He, too, my friend, is guilty of whatever she is. The whole of Cachtice and Sarvar are bloody cursed. Bathory's cousin Count George Thurzo has been appointed to head up the investigation," Meldritch explained. "Dozens and dozens of testimonies from all over."

"Well, if there is no war here, perhaps I shall return home," Smith said.

"I heard there is an ongoing war in Africa, Captain Smith, if that suits your plans," Meldritch said.

"I believe I will head to Venice and perhaps find some new adventure, whether it be on the Barbary Coast or back to England," Smith said.

"Stay a few more days, build your strength, gather your provisions, and plot your course. It is a long way to Venice. This time, we will ensure you have more than corn to eat."

Both men shared a laugh as they sipped on Italian wine and ate merrily throughout the night.

Chapter 26 - Where Shadows Dare to Run

It was the midnight hour, and Castle Cachtice lay shrouded in an eerie stillness. The last of the day's noises had faded, leaving only the soft rustle of leaves in the distant woods. A few lone guards, half-asleep and inattentive, patrolled the castle's perimeter, their footsteps muffled by the thick stone walls and the cloak of darkness. The late winter's night was quiet, the winds barely whispering as if nature held its breath. Above, the sky stretched wide and clear, an endless blanket of stars shimmering like scattered diamonds.

Inside the castle, everything was peaceful, too peaceful. The halls were bathed in moonlight, the silence broken only by the occasional creak of old timber settling in one of the roof structures. The inhabitants of Cachtice lay in deep, undisturbed slumber, unaware of the two figures quietly preparing for their final departure.

"Tonight is the night," Peter said. "Let's make our preparations."

"I'm ready," Margaret said.

"I will be across the hall. Come when you are ready," Peter whispered.

Peter crept back across the hall, while Margaret put on her newly made travel dress and gathered what little she had. She looked around her room one last time and crept across the hall to her father's quarters. She carefully opened the door, making sure not to make too much noise, as sound echoed tremendously through the stone hallways.

"Are you ready?" Peter asked.

"No," Margaret said. "I don't want to die."

"You are not going to die, my love. We are leaving this place, once and for all: no more skimpy meals, bloody murders, or putrid decomposition. We are leaving these witches and vampires behind," Peter said. "Remember, I am here with you, every step of the way."

Peter threw his heavy satchel of gold and other belongings over his shoulder and threw on a dark cowl to cloak him in the darkness.

"We have gone over this a thousand times. Remember to follow my lead."

"Yes, Father."

Peter and Margaret opened the chamber door and looked down the dark hallway for any sign of movement.

"Come on," Peter whispered.

The two barefoot Dowlings crept along the walls, each step being as careful and intentional as possible. They reached the top of the staircase and began to tiptoe, one stone step at a time.

It was dark except for a lone candle flickering by the front entrance. Peter scanned the area for any sign of movement. He knew two guards patrolled the grounds overnight, one inside and one outside. The two armed guards would switch patrols several times throughout the frigid nights.

Peter and Margaret were almost invisible as they reached the bottom of the steps. They both began moving along the corridor towards the door when Peter noticed a guard walking through the dining hall to their right. Peter flung his hand in front of Margaret, and they both froze as the guard disappeared into the next room.

They stealthily approached the large oak doors and carefully unlatched the two deadbolts. This noise would likely be the most risky part of their escape. Peter stuck his foot under the door to help ease the tension on the hinges. Inch by inch, the door opened, letting the frigid winter winds pour into the castle. Margaret shuffled outside, followed by Peter. He quickly and delicately closed the door, and they made their way along the castle wall to the stable.

Outside the stable, they paused to put on their boots.

"You are doing great so far," Peter whispered.

"I'm scared, Father," Margaret replied.

"The hard part is over," Peter said. "Now, let's get inside the stable."

Margaret opened the latch, and they both slipped inside the wooden stable. Peter immediately grabbed a hanging saddle and threw it over the top of a drowsy black horse awoken by the subtle commotion of their entrance. Peter buckled and tied down the heavy saddle, then found the bridle for the horse's head and began buckling it gently.

Margaret opened the other stable doors leading to the path out of the castle. The doors were significantly heavier than she thought. "I need help," Margaret muttered.

"Right," Peter said, as he stroked the horse's cheek to establish a bond with the animal.

"Hurry!" Margaret's anxiety was rising.

Peter ran and helped open the large doors. "Come on!" he said, grabbing Margaret by the hand.

Peter opened the horse's gate, led the giant stallion out of the stall, put his foot in the stirrup and mounted the unfamiliar animal. He then pulled his daughter up behind him.

"Ready?" Peter asked.

"Yes," Margaret said. "I hope you know what you're doing."

Peter gently dug his heels into the horse, and it began to trot out through the barn and down the path. The cloaked riders trotted out of the stable and down the gravel path leading to the road down the mountain. The horse's trot was loud and echoed against the stone walls. The horse began to pick up speed under the starry, moonlit sky.

"So far, so good," Peter said.

The riders descended through the main gate of Castle Cachtice, which stood wide open, a testament to the bustle of activity and the fragile peace newly forged between neighbouring kingdoms. Both Peter and Margaret knew the urgency of their escape. Riding through the night was their only hope of putting as much distance as possible between themselves and the castle. The Countess would undoubtedly be furious, and her soldiers would quickly follow.

Once they reached the mountain base, their pace quickened from a trot to a steady gallop. The horse, eager to stretch his legs, seemed to find a new sense of ease as the terrain levelled out. With each mile, the looming silhouette of Castle Cachtice grew smaller, and the weight on their shoulders eased.

The crisp, cool air wrapped around them like a refreshing embrace, perfect for the long ride ahead. The pine forests mingled with the sharp bite of winter, filling their lungs with each breath. The night felt heavier, more ominous, and somehow more intimate, as if the world had drawn in close to witness their escape.

Soon, the first few flakes of snow began to drift down, barely noticeable at first, but as the minutes passed, the snow became a steady cascade that clung to their hair, clothes, and horses' hooves.

Peter's eyes flickered upward, watching the snowflakes swirl in the night air. He could feel the moment's weight pressing on him, but calm settled over him. The snow was their ally now, nature's own cloak of secrecy. "God is watching over us," Peter murmured. He looked ahead, watching the landscape blur through the snow. "This will cover our tracks."

Margaret squeezed her father tightly; her arms wrapped around his waist as the horse surged forward. Her heart pounded in her chest, not from fear but from the pure, intoxicating joy of the freedom they desperately sought.

She looked over her shoulder, her gaze catching the distant silhouette of the castle, now fading into the dark behind them. The castle that had once felt like a cage, a place of restriction and oppression, now felt distant and foreign.

"She's finally gone," Margaret said.

Peter's face remained hard, his eyes sharp and focused on the road ahead. "We're not out of the woods yet," he replied, his tone a mix of pragmatism and the underlying tension that still held him. He couldn't allow himself to relax. The night was still young, and danger lurked in every shadow. But for the first time in what felt like forever, a small part of him dared to believe they might make it out alive.

"Faster, father, faster!" Margaret yelled into the night, her voice a joyous cry that echoed off the distant trees, carried away by the wind.

The night would be long, and the journey perilous. But for now, with the snow swirling around them and the wind at their backs, it felt like the world was opening up in front of them, a world they could claim once again.

"Hold tight!" Peter yelled.

Peter flung the reins, and the horse's pace quickened. Margaret's face glowed with hope and determination as they entered the Village of Cachtice.

Chapter 27 - A Gift From Above

The harsh, jarring bangs on the door echoed through the stillness of Elizabeth Bathory's opulent bedroom, shaking her from the depths of a restless sleep. Her eyes flew open, and her body stiffened with the shock of being pulled from the dark corners of her dreams. The noise was deafening, loud, insistent, and so intrusive that it felt as though the very walls of her castle were reverberating with cannon fire. For a moment, she lay there, frozen, her blood boiling with indignation.

"What do you want?" she screamed with a venomous hiss.

The response came immediately, though muffled through the thick oak door, the tone faltering under the weight of her fury. "My Lady. My Lady, it is Mr. Dowling and his daughter. They appear to have fled the castle on horseback."

The words hit her like a physical blow. Her body went rigid. For a heartbeat, Elizabeth sat there, the enormity of the situation sinking into her bones. Her mind processed the implications with a cold, calculating, violent precision. Peter Dowling, that bastard, dared defy her. Fleeing her castle in the dead of night. How could they? How dare they?

Her fists clenched harder, nails digging into the flesh of her palms as she forced herself to stand. As she rose, the bed creaked under her weight, her movements fluid but charged with an anger so pure and raw it could have consumed her whole.

"Gather my riders," she commanded, her voice suddenly low. "I will be downstairs in a moment."

"Yes, my Lady," came the hesitant reply, and retreating footsteps echoed in the corridor.

Elizabeth did not wait another second. Her mind was a maelstrom, whirling with rage, betrayal, and humiliation. How could they escape her? How could they think they could outrun her? She would inflict the cruellest torture upon their capture.

Without thinking, she kicked her nightstand, smashing a lantern, sending wax and glass everywhere. With a primal scream, Elizabeth tore the nearest painting from the wall, its frame splintering beneath her fingers as she flung it across the room. The delicate oil portrait of a long-dead ancestor collided with the stone. But still, it was not enough. The rage that boiled in her veins, hot and dangerous, could not be satisfied with a few broken trinkets. It needed more.

With another scream that echoed through the castle's cavernous halls, Elizabeth turned toward the heavy mirror hanging on the opposite wall. The reflection that stared back at her was a twisted, fury-driven vision of herself, her eyes broad with madness, her face flushed with anger. She charged toward it; her hands raised in a frenzy of destruction. But something strange happened as her fingers made contact with the cold, polished surface. Her own reflection seemed to flicker. The rage that had consumed her, that had been her sole driving force for so long, paused just for a moment.

For that brief, fleeting instant, she saw herself not as the powerful, regal woman she had once been, but as the twisted, broken creature she had become. She saw the monster in the mirror, the one who had drowned in her own vices, the one who had pushed everyone and everything away until there was only the cold stone of Castle Cachtice and her relentless thirst for blood and vengeance.

But the moment passed, and the fragile flicker of doubt vanished. With a booming roar, Elizabeth swung her hand into the mirror, her fist crashing through the glass with a deafening shatter.

Peter and Margaret rode through the night, through the Village of Cachtice, past the Kovacs household, and into the rocky, barren landscape of the Carpathian Mountains.

Weariness set in as the Dowlings pressed on through the night, and the excitement eventually wore off. Peter realized the horse needed a short rest, so they led the animal down into a forested, unsuspecting valley with a small stream running through the middle. The horse was exhausted, drank its fill of spring water, and found a few patches of dead grass beneath the snowy terrain.

"We can only sleep for a few hours, as the dragon Countess is not far behind," Peter said. "I will wake you when we're ready."

"Yes, Father," Margaret said as she wrapped herself in the wool cloak and closed her eyes.

Peter did not sleep at all. He leaned against a tree and looked up at the falling snow, ready to move instantly.

Countess Bathory made her way down the cold stone steps toward her dungeon. She intended to focus on something that gave her immediate pleasure and satisfaction, rather than continue to dwell on her indignation towards Peter and

Margaret. She had sent a dozen riders to track down the Dowlings and bring them back alive.

Elizabeth opened the dungeon door and stepped inside, closing and latching the door behind her. The foul stench did not bother her anymore. The decaying effluvium permeated through the cold, rusty cells. One dead girl lay hanging and decomposing from the iron handcuffs cemented in the wall. In a corner of the far cell, two bodies were piled on top of one another. Rats scurried around all corners of the dungeon.

One girl, barely hanging on to life, bound by the wrists, slowly opened her eyes to the Countess standing at the gate of her cell.

"I'm thirsty," Bathory coldly said.

"Please, have mercy," the dishevelled girl said.

"I do not have a drop of mercy in me. That is all gone now. The peace is gone; the happiness, the sympathy. Your blood and sacrifice are for the benefit of this kingdom. Your blood will soothe the wounds of my broken heart."

"You don't have to do this," the girl pleaded.

"Yes, my dear, I do," Bathory replied.

Bathory's twelve armed horsemen rode in the Village of Cachtice in the early morning light. With the six inches of snow, the riders were aimless in pursuing Peter and Margaret. The riders split up and weaved between properties, looking for a black horse, or any other clue that might lead them to the deserters.

One rider approached the home of the Kovacs family and saw their little boy, Sam, playing in the snow.

"You there, boy!" the rider yelled. "Go get your mother and father!" he said, dismounting his horse.

Little Sam ran inside, and a few moments later, a weary Jan and Catharine stepped outside in the blowing wind and gusting snow.

"We have two deserters on the loose," the horseman said. "We are in pursuit of Peter Dowling and his daughter. Have you seen these individuals in the last twelve hours?"

"No, sir, we have not," Jan quickly said. "We will keep a keen eye on the fields for them."

The horseman, without hesitation, walked between Jan and Catharine and through the front door of their home. He turned up mattresses, lifted furniture, and even stole a piece of bread from the kitchen counter.

"Have you seen our daughter? Maria?" Catharine pleaded with the horseman.

"Girls come and go quickly at the Bathory residence," the horseman said.

"She sings; she plays the organ. We have not heard from her in months. She promised to write to us every few weeks; it's not like her to ignore her family," Catharine said.

The rider paused, chewing on his bread. "Ah, yes," he said, spitting his mouthful to the ground. There was a long pause. "Your daughter Maria plays music for the Countess night and day. The Countess enjoys her melodies and inspires her hobbies," the rider said, walking out the door. "I must be on my way; send word to the magistrate should you find Peter and Margaret Dowling. The Countess is not pleased."

"We will," Jan and Catharine said as the rider mounted his horse.

Pastor Istivan was jogging down the snowy road and stopped Elizabeth's horseman in the middle of the dirt road. He threw up his hands and waved frantically. "Stop! By God, stop!" he yelled.

"Christ Almighty, what do you want, Pastor?" the horseman said.

"I have just seen your escapees!" Istivan said.

"By God, where?" the rider inquired.

"Heading east towards the river, on the road out of town, running swift and hard. Two riders, one horse," Istivan said, slightly out of breath.

The horseman nodded at Pastor Istivan, dug his heels into his horse, and galloped away.

Once out of eyesight, the out-of-breath Pastor smiled at Maria's parents.

"Why do you tell these spawns of the devil where they are riding? Have you no faith, Pastor?" Catharine yelled.

"Those people were riding for their lives, running from the devil herself," Jan followed.

Pastor Istivan urged them to calm down with his hands. He put his index finger to his mouth. "The riders were heading due west, not east," Istivan said, smiling and pointing in the opposite direction from where he had just sent the horseman. "All is right in heaven and hell."

"You clever man!" Jan said, laughing.

After a brief pause, Catharine pleaded, "Pastor, things are getting worse in Castle Cachtice. Our daughter is still there, and we have not heard a word in months."

"Mrs. Kovacs, Mr. Kovacs, I have brought word of Bathory's sinister actions before Count Thurzo, and he promises to deliver justice. King Matthias is now in control and is a person of action, unlike the unassertive complacency of Emperor Rudolph. It should not be too long until the heinous woman is brought to justice."

Pastor Istivan's words were comforting to Mr. and Mrs. Kovacs. It seemed that words were finally being put into action after what seemed like decades of missing and murdered girls.

"Thank you, Pastor," Catharine said.

"I shall see you Sunday," Istivan said with a smile.

"Goodbye, Pastor," Jan said. "Let God bless our baby Maria."

"God bless you and your child," the Pastor said as he departed.

—William Mowat—

Chapter 28 - Venice

After days of hard riding from the Earl's estate in Transylvania, Captain Smith finally arrived in Venice. He spent a week indulging in the city's pleasures: eating well, drinking freely, and wandering its canal-lined streets. But the thrill of leisure soon gave way to restlessness. His adventurous spirit meant he had no desire to return to England, so he lingered by the busy docks, looking for opportunity. One by one, he approached various captains, mercenaries, traders, and pirates alike, offering his services to any crew that might value a seasoned soldier with a taste for danger.

Eventually, he found a French adventurer who wanted to head to the Barbary Coast. However, after discovering the feudal nature of the situation, Smith and the Frenchman decided to avoid the conflict altogether.

After a few aimless weeks at sea, Smith returned to Venice and began searching for a passage back to England. Though disappointed he hadn't found work that matched his skills, a quiet longing for home had begun to take hold. Something told him England might soon need men like him. Now 25, a veteran of many battles, Smith sensed that his story was far from over. In fact, he believed his true adventure was only just beginning.

The young Captain Smith approached a ship docked in Venice flying England's new Union Jack flag. At first, he did not recognize the flag but remembered hearing about the pattern from a fellow English soldier in Wallachia. He smiled proudly at his homeland's new colours and approached the ship.

"Hello there!" Smith yelled to the quarter deck.

"That sounds like an English accent!" the Captain roared back.

"Pardon my interruption, but I am seeking a ride to England," Smith said. "I was wondering if you were heading there anytime soon."

"This is rather odd, but there seem to be stray Englishmen all over these docks. I just agreed to sail another gentleman home. Captain Merham is my name," he said, shaking Smith's hand.

"Captain Merham, it is a pleasure to meet you. It has been a long time since I've heard that beautiful Elizabethan accent," Smith said. "John Smith at your service, Captain John Smith."

"You must be returning from the war against the Turks?" Merham asked. "A lot of you blokes passing through here. Some with arms missing, some with legs missing, a lot of horrible scars."

"We all have terrible scars, Captain," Smith said.

"Where are yours?" Merham inquired.

Smith pulled his shirt over his head and revealed the dozens of scars from Crimean whips across his back.

"Golly," Merham said. "You were a slave?"

"In Crimea for a period, on a wheat farm with the vilest of Tatars."

"How did you get your Captaincy, if you don't mind my prying?" Merham asked.

"Earned in Hungary. A series of three contests brought about some riches, fame, and my captaincy."

"The war was pretty hard, wasn't it?" Merham asked.

"It was a long, hard few years, full of bloodshed, adventure, and turmoil, but the Sultan and Emperor reached a peace agreement some months back, so here I am, Captain John Smith, looking for a ride back to merry England."

"Well, Smith, it is great to have another able set of hands on board," Merham said. "Funny, you're an Englishman. Not two days ago, a father and daughter approached me and asked for a ride to England."

Merham stuck his head through the door to the crew's quarters. "Hey-o! Dowling! On deck!"

From the crew's quarters emerged Peter Dowling, clean-shaven and well-dressed.

"Ah, here we are, speak of the devil," Merham said. "Here is Mr. Dowling, the other Englishman I spoke about."

Peter and Smith stared at each other, slowly realizing they recognized one another.

"Mr. Dowling?" Smith was shocked.

"Little John Smith?" Peter responded. "What on earth are you doing here?"

"Returning to England," Smith said, hugging Peter.

"Me too!"

Merham stood confused at the entire situation.

"Where have you been?" Peter asked. "What brings you here?"

"Fighting the Turks in Hungary," Smith responded. "Now I'm here looking for a way home. What about you?"

"I was tutoring in Hungary!" Peter answered. "Left grammar school for the promise of big riches in Prague."

"That is incredible," Smith said.

"So, judging by what I've seen, you two must know each other?" Merham said, cheekily.

"I used to teach this little boy at King Edward VI Grammar School in Louth. Last I had heard, you were set on a path to apprentice with a merchant in Norfolk," Peter said, grabbing Smith around the shoulder. Dowling had taught young John in the 1590s and reflected on his pupil's energetic behaviour and courageous nature.

"Mr. Dowling was new to the profession, but he was a great mentor and leader," Smith said to Merham. "Ultimately, I set aside my mercantilism and education and became a soldier under the Earl of Meldritch in Transylvania."

"Unbelievable," Peter said. "My daughter and I were under contract with Elizabeth Bathory in Transylvania, throughout these past years."

"Elizabeth and Ferenc Nadasdy?" Smith asked in disbelief.

"Yes, at the Castle Cachtice," Peter answered.

"Ferenc and I fought side by side throughout my time in Hungary and Transylvania," Smith said, shaking his head in disbelief.

"After Ferenc died, Elizabeth spun right out of control. Very messy situation at that castle. A lot of innocent blood is being spilt." Peter reflected on the gruesome, horrific image of the young, dead, naked girl who froze to death in the courtyard of Castle Cachtice. "The Countess is out of control. The clergy, local villages, and magistrates are aware of her actions. I feared for our lives, so my daughter and I escaped in the midnight hour without injury. There are still many young girls trapped within her stone walls. I am just hoping they can somehow be saved."

"Ferenc was a ruthless soldier and quite fond of torturing his captives. So it does not surprise me that Elizabeth took a shine to his fancy," Smith said.

"Well, I'm glad we are all now acquainted," Merham said, intervening with a toothless smile. "Shall we have a drink?"

"I do not object," Smith said.

"Nor I," Dowling said.

All three men laughed and moved below deck as the sun set on the beautiful city of Venice.

—William Mowat—

Chapter 29 – A Deep Scar

Elizabeth and her three servants, Dorka, Illona, and Helena, sat outside around a small wooden table drinking tea. It was early spring, and bugs hummed and buzzed throughout the mountains. It was a dull, overcast day as Fitzko, the small, ugly dwarf, escorted another young girl before the Countess and her servants.

Fitzko, without hesitation, tore off her dress, leaving the girl completely naked. He promptly told the girl to lie down with her arms and legs spread apart. Fitzko proceeded to stake her to the ground, bound by the wrists with hemp rope.

"Stay still, little girl," Fitzko said, drooling over the terrified girl.

"Oh, be nice to the girl," Elizabeth said unconvincingly.

Once the girl was secured to the ground, he went back inside, and a moment later, he returned with a bucket and a ladle. He placed the bucket on the tea table and bowed to his master.

"Well done, Fitzko. That was almost as entertaining as me slitting that girl's tongue from her mouth last week," the Countess said.

The Countess rose from her seat, grabbed the bucket, and approached the helpless girl.

"Please, don't kill me!" the poor naked girl feebly said.

"I'm not going to kill you, darling," Elizabeth said with a villainous smile. Elizabeth began to smother the naked girl with honey. She dripped the resinous substance all along her body and spread it with the ladle. "I'm not going to be the one who kills you," she said, laughing.

Bugs almost immediately started to land on the girl and get stuck in the honey. Elizabeth had learned this gruesome tactic from Helena. The death was never immediate, but slow and torturous. Welts, bumps, and bruises would continually develop, then once the sores opened up, the mice and rats would begin their feast.

Elizabeth was taken back to her youth as she reminisced about her uncle sewing the thief inside the horse carcass. It was transporting, as she watched the initial struggle of the girl morph into passive helplessness. Her power and control over life were intoxicating and lifted her spirit.

Bugs began to swarm all over the girl's body. With each new bite, her body would slightly twitch, and she would scream. As the hours passed, her eyes became swollen shut, and welts appeared over her entire body, and the screams stopped.

Elizabeth would return the next day to find the girl struggling to hold onto life. The Countess gave her a nudge with her foot, and the dirty, swollen girl could only moan as a few field mice scurried out from under her.

"Your sacrifice is for the greater good of the Kingdom of Hungary. Your example will provide an important lesson for those who surround you. May you travel well, darling," Elizabeth said as she returned inside.

On the third day of the girl's torture, she was found dead early in the morning. The body was covered in dirt and blood, and it was being eaten from the inside out. Rats, mice, and other creatures burrowed inside her torso and animated her body as if she were still alive.

After a few more days of visiting the corpse and seeing the progression of decomposition, Elizabeth had ordered the body to be tossed over the castle wall, down into the ravine where the wolves would finish the job.

Fitzko and Dorka disposed of the girl and looked down into the ravine, where a half dozen more dead bodies lay across the ground in various states of rigor mortis. Fitzko knew the bodies and the smells were becoming a problem and pondered what the grim future of Castle Cachtice might be.

—William Mowat—

Chapter 30 - The Saint George

Captain Merham's ship, called the St. George, had sailed through the Mediterranean and arrived in the port of Saffi, off the coast of Morocco. As the St. George rolled into port, black skies appeared, with hurricane-force winds, and the St. George was unable to dock.

"Secure the deck, reef the sails!" Merham yelled on deck.

"Aye, Captain!" sailors yelled.

"We're going to need to slip the cable!" Merham yelled again. "We're not going to outrun this storm. We're going to ride it out!"

John Smith and Peter Dowling emerged to help all they could, while Margaret Dowling did her best to secure items below deck.

"How now, Captain Smith! Mr. Dowling! Look at the beast that approaches!" Merham yelled.

The skies began to open, and the rains fell heavily and hard. The waves became turbulent as the winds pushed the St. George further and further away from shore.

"Feels like good English weather!" John Smith yelled.

Merham gave a good chuckle. "Not exactly the warm Moroccan weather we were looking for."

"Are we just looking to ride it out?" Peter asked.

"This storm will probably carry us to the Canary Islands!" Merham said. "We will head offshore until we can raise sail and maintain course!"

After hours of black skies and torrential downpours, the St. George did drift as far as Merham had predicted. The Canary Islands were a tropical paradise, but the Captain and his crew didn't have time to rest and explore the islands. As a group, Merham and his crew had decided to find some privateers to rob. They would look for any ship worthy of boarding and rob it.

The morning after the storm, the St. George set sail and eventually ran alongside a small Portuguese schooner that would be ripe for the taking.

"Lower your mainsail, or we will open fire!" Merham yelled.

"We don't want any trouble!" the Portuguese Captain hollered.

"Then lower that sail!" Merham responded.

The Portuguese Captain knew it was not in his best interest to try to fight the bigger, faster ship with twice his crew. Eventually, the boat came to a stop.

"Reel her in!" Merham said as his crew threw grappling hooks over the side of the Portuguese boat.

"We only have wine bound for Teneriffe!" the Portuguese captain said.

"We will be happy to relieve that from you," Merham said with a beaming smile.

Peter Dowling turned to Captain John Smith. "I've had all the adventures I can handle."

"I think this adventure is just getting started," Smith said, winking at Peter.

Chapter 31 - Silence in Cachtice

Elizabeth Bathory was slowly deteriorating, her once regal and formidable presence now a shadow of its former self. Her health had declined so rapidly that even the most loyal servants could no longer ignore its toll on her. The sickness that gripped her body seemed to leach away her vitality from the inside out, draining all her strength and energy. The fever had taken hold, and her epileptic seizures had increased and worsened with each passing day, rendering her bedridden and weak.

Once, her room had been filled with the luxurious scents of candles and perfumes, and the rich tapestries hung in heavy silence. It smelled faintly of decay and sickness, like the walls had begun to erode with her.

The nights that were the hardest for her to endure. Sleep, or what passed for sleep in her condition, was a refuge she could no longer reach alone. Once sharp and cunning, her mind had become clouded with confusion, lost in a fog of fever dreams and waking nightmares. Every night, she found herself calling for Maria, the soft-voiced servant girl, to come and sing her lullabies, those old, familiar songs that used to lull her into a peaceful, uninterrupted slumber. Now, they merely served as a temporary escape, a brief moment of calm in a world that seemed to slip further from her grasp.

Elizabeth lay propped up in her bed, her face pale and drawn. Her dark hair, once a crown of beauty, now hung limp around her shoulders, unkempt. She looked smaller now, as though the very essence of her power was being slowly drained from her frame. The years of cruelty and excess had taken their toll, and now there was little left of the infamous Countess Bathory except a broken woman, consumed by illness and loneliness.

"Dorka!" Elizabeth's voice cracked in the room's stillness, calling out to her most trusted servant.

The door creaked open, and Dorka stepped into the room, her presence starkly contrasting to the fragile woman lying in bed. Dorka was sturdy, solid, and loyal to the end. Elizabeth's once imperious demands had grown weaker, more pleading. Her once fearsome beauty was now a faded memory, and Dorka could not help but notice how her mistress had become a prisoner of her own body.

"My Lady?" Dorka's voice was gentle but firm, her eyes scanning the room before resting on Elizabeth, struggling to sit up.

Elizabeth's thin fingers gripped the bedpost as she made another attempt to push herself upright.

"You need to rest, my Lady," Dorka urged, moving swiftly to her side to help her back down.

"Nonsense," Elizabeth muttered. "My husband needs me."

Dorka froze at the mention of Ferenc, Elizabeth's long-dead husband. She could feel a pang of sorrow deep in her chest, for it had been many years since his death; years that had seen Elizabeth's reign grow darker, more twisted, and more isolated. Ferenc was gone, and Elizabeth's mind seemed to wander the halls of memory, grasping at fleeting moments of a past she could no longer hold.

"Ferenc is gone, my Lady," Dorka replied softly. "Gone many years now."

Elizabeth blinked slowly, as if trying to process the words. Her confusion settled like a heavy fog over her face, but she struggled to focus. "Where are my children?" she muttered.

"They are in Prague, my Lady. You sent Paul to grammar school just recently. They are safe."

The room seemed to close around the Countess, and a strange sense of vulnerability took root in her heart. The children she had once fiercely protected now seemed like distant figures, their lives unfolding far from her castle walls.

"Where is Mr. Dowling and his lovely daughter?" Elizabeth asked, utterly exhausted.

Dorka's expression hardened, but she did not falter. "They're gone, my Liege. They escaped. Our riders reported that they are headed west, toward Poland."

"Escaped?" Elizabeth moaned, her voice trembling with a mix of disbelief and frustration. Her mind tried to grasp the implications, but the fever fog blurred her thoughts. "How did that happen?"

"Perhaps it was just their time to leave," Dorka said gently, her tone softening as she stepped back. "Now, please, go back to sleep, my Lady. You need rest. You need to heal."

The room was still for a moment, and Dorka stood there, watching her dozing mistress. The once-feared Countess, whose name had been synonymous with cruelty and power, was now a broken shell, haunted by her past and gripped by the decay of her body.

As Dorka turned to leave, her mind lingered on the strange, unsettling truth that had settled in the air around them.

—William Mowat—

The castle, once a symbol of the Bathory family's strength and might, had become a tomb for the victims of Elizabeth's cruelty and for Elizabeth herself. She had ruled with fear, but now she was a prisoner to her own mortality. Dorka closed the door quietly behind her with one last glance at her mistress.

Chapter 32 - The Man-of-War

"Ahoy! Four points off our starboard bow!" Merham's 1st mate, Reginald Mercer, yelled.

"Show me, Mr. Mercer," Captain Merham said.

Merham peered through the looking glass. "Damn. A Spanish man-of-war. Twice our guns, twice our men."

"What is your plan, Captain?" Captain John Smith asked, overhearing the conversation.

"We are going to try and outrun her," Merham said. "Let's see if we can cover ourselves in darkness before she catches up."

"Shall I prepare for engagement below deck, Captain?" Smith asked.

"Get those guns stuffed with grapeshot, anything to cause damage to her rigging and hull," Merham said. "Wait for my word, Smith."

"Aye, Captain," Smith said as he ran below deck.

Arriving on the gun deck, John Smith called Peter Dowling over and described the current situation on the water. "We need you to prepare the infirmary with Dr. Fairfax, Mr. Dowling. Take your daughter with you. Protect her and have her help if need be. It's a man-of-war, and fighting will likely get intimate."

Peter grabbed Margaret by the hand and helped Dr. Fairfax set up his small infirmary. There was a table, crude surgical tools, and a lone bucket of water.

"We are going to need your hands, Mr. Dowling," Fairfax said.

"My daughter and I are at your service," Peter responded.

Above deck, Merham knew he was overmatched, and the Spaniards were almost within firing range.

"Prepare for battle!" Merham yelled.

The first rounds of cannons erupted from the man-of-war landing just off the port side of the British frigate.

"Hold course!" Merham yelled.

The second round of cannon balls struck the rigging of the main mast and sent cleats and rope flying everywhere. The main sails began to crinkle and drop to the deck.

"Hollins, Moffat, on the main mast!" Merham yelled.

The Spanish ship was only a few feet from launching a broadside strike against Merham's boat.

"Captain Smith! Now!" Merham yelled at the top of his lungs.

"Fire!" Smith yelled to his gun crews.

Each blast hit the man-of-war but did minor damage. The last cannon, which Smith had personally packed with iron bolts and crossbars, was lit. The resulting explosion blew a hole in the hull of the man-of-war. Water began pouring into the Spanish ship, with the boats now only feet away.

Both sides threw their grappling irons, and the firefight began. Musket balls flew between ships as hand-to-hand combat followed. Frantic swords clashing, and axes dropping through the thick fog of gun smoke, confused both sides, as the

Spanish frantically began repairing the massive hole in their boat.

Smith ordered his gun crew to pick up rifles and follow him to the quarter deck, where they aimed at the massive sail above the Spanish troops. Dozens of shots destroyed the hinges carrying the weight of the sails as the main sail fell on top of a hundred or so men.

"Reload and fire!" Smith roared.

Through the mayhem, Merham noticed the progress on his rigging and the clever tactics of John Smith, and felt an urge of confidence pass through him. "Heavy fire on that sail!" he yelled.

The Spanish lost dozens of men, but still had superior numbers.

The first wounded began rolling into the infirmary. Dr. Fairfax was already sweating as the first patient was put up on the table with a bullet wound to the arm.

"Hold him down, Mr. Dowling," Fairfax said, picking up his clamps.

"Bite down on this," Margaret said, putting a small piece of wood in his mouth.

"Be brave, soldier," Fairfax said as he plunged the clamps into the bullet wound.

Above deck, the Spanish began overtaking the British frigate's mid-deck. Merham's men still controlled both the high grounds of the stern and bow, as Captain Smith devised a plan.

He rolled a barrel of gunpowder right underneath the midship, urged everyone away from the mid-deck, and lit the fuse.

With a thunderous clap, the barrel blew straight up, sending dozens of Spaniards to their death. In the confused aftermath, the British sailors could unclasp most of the grappling hooks and disengage with the man-of-war.

The Spanish Captain was so demoralized by the sudden loss of so many men and the damage done to his ship that he decided to break off the attack.

As the two ships parted, they continued blasting cannon shots at one another until they were out of eyesight.

Below deck, dozens were saved thanks to the medical actions and thinking of Dr. Fairfax, Peter, and Margaret Dowling. There had been burn victims, bullet wounds, and the amputation of one Brit's leg, which a cannon blast had blown apart. Blood was everywhere, and eventually, they could clean down the surfaces with buckets of seawater.

"Well done, Mr. Dowling, Miss Dowling. Splendid work. You have saved a lot of lives today," Fairfax said.

"Excellent job yourself, Dr. Fairfax," Peter said.

Captain Merham thanked everyone for their superb effort against superior guns and manpower, especially John Smith's quick thinking.

"Though you blew up half my ship and set fire to her, I thank you for your actions today, Captain Smith," Merham said. "Let's take this crippled ship back to Saffi and undergo some urgent repairs."

"Aye, Captain. Home indeed," Smith said.

On the way back to the Moroccan port city of Saffi, Captain Smith reflected on his journey for adventure and fame. He had come close to death on so many occasions and thanked God for still being alive.

Peter arrived on the main deck and saw Smith looking at the horizon.

"Well done, Captain Smith," Peter said, approaching the dirty soldier.

"Well, hello there, Mr. Dowling, sir," Smith responded. "Glad to see you're still in one piece."

"I can't believe we survived that ordeal," Peter said, looking at the gaping hole in the mid-deck.

"Certainly was a desperate act, at a desperate time," Smith said. "I've survived so many of these sea-faring engagements, I've lost count."

"Well, you are a soldier, that is for certain," Peter said. "Perhaps it is time you look somewhere else for adventure. Somewhere with fewer cannons."

"What are you suggesting, Mr. Dowling?" Smith asked.

"I'm not quite sure, John. But you are meant for something greater than dying on a ship by flying wooden splinters. Perhaps, it is time for a return home." Peter said, looking north, towards England.

—William Mowat—

Chapter 33 - A Grandiose Feast

Countess Bathory, ever the mistress of grandeur and intrigue, decided to host the most extravagant dinner party her castle had ever seen. The occasion was twofold: a triumphant celebration marking the end of the bloody conflict with the Ottoman Empire, and the dawn of a new era under the freshly crowned King Matthias, heralding the rebirth of the Kingdom of Hungary.

After several weeks of recovery and rest, the Countess had gathered her strength and reignited her former self. She needed to re-establish her position and status in the kingdom. All the nobles from miles around would be at the celebration. No expense was to be spared. With a passion for excess, the Countess poured vast sums of gold into preparing a feast worthy of royalty and legend. Her various servants were dispatched across the countryside and beyond, returning with an abundance of livestock: twelve plump goats, four grown steers, one hundred chickens, and twenty turkeys. From the distant orchards of the Mediterranean came crates of exotic fruits: pomegranates, figs, citrus, and dates, their colours vibrant and their fragrances intoxicating.

Her income had dwindled since her husband's passing, but Elizabeth's appetite for decadence had not faltered. Though groaning under the strain, the castle treasury still flowed freely at her command. She believed appearances mattered more than balance sheets, and in the treacherous world of nobility, she needed to reinstate her high-status command and position; then the gold would follow.

In the coming weeks, leading up to the grand affair, the castle grounds would be a whirlwind of preparation. Every stone, every crevice would be scoured by hand. Under threat of the Countess's wrath, the servants laboured day and night to scrub the ancient flagstones and smoke-darkened walls with ammonia, lavender oil, and lime.

However, the darker corners of the castle required a more sinister cleansing. The torture chamber, nestled in the damp depths of the dungeons, had long been a silent witness to unspeakable horrors. It, too, was scrubbed clean of the blood and guts. The bodies, many already decaying, were unceremoniously removed, carted away under the cover of night and burned in the woods beyond the castle walls.

Inside the newly cleaned and decorated castle, young Maria Kovacs was summoned to the main floor library of Castle Cachtice, where Elizabeth waited patiently. Young Maria arrived and curtsied to the Countess. "Hello, my Lady," she said, looking at the ground.

"You are quite the celebrity around the castle, young Miss Kovacs," Elizabeth said as she approached Maria.

"Thank you, my Lady. I have done my best to please your highness," Maria said.

"And you have pleased me greatly," Elizabeth said, running her hands through her long, brown hair. "You have restored faith in me. You have reminded me that I am in control."

Maria thought how strange it was for the Countess to be so kind. It was so unlike her.

"You are to prepare a few hours of music for our special guests next month. Much is going into the preparations of this occasion, and I expect you to be at your best," Elizabeth said.

"I promise to give my absolute best," Maria said. "You will not be disappointed."

"It is so wonderful to hear you say that," the Countess said. "I have a surprise for you." Bathory retrieved a parcel tied with a string from a nearby desk. "Open your gift."

"For me, you shouldn't have," Maria said.

"Nonsense," Elizabeth said.

Maria carefully removed the string from the parcel and unwrapped the gift, revealing the crimson dress the Countess had bought her in Prague. Maria held up the dress, and her eyes lit up as she scanned the delicate embroidery and lace details. "It is beautiful, my Lady. I cannot believe how lovely it is."

"Made of the finest eastern silk. It should be a perfect fit. You and I are around the same size," the Countess said with a genuine smile.

"My sincerest gratitude, Countess," Maria said.

"I expect you to wear this dress at the celebration when you are performing for our guests," Bathory said.

"I will, I promise," Maria immediately responded.

"I will call on you regularly to ensure you are ready," Elizabeth said. "Now, you are excused."

"Yes, my Lady," Maria said, as she left smiling at her new dress.

Having done something thoughtful and genuine for somebody else, Elizabeth felt a surge of happiness course through her body and mind, an alien feeling that somehow left her feeling fulfilled.

—William Mowat—

—1599: Empires of Blood—

Chapter 34 - Along the Thames

Captain Merham and his battered ship finally limped into the sheltered harbour of Sappi, a bustling Moroccan port known as much for its colourful bazaars as its strategic importance along the Mediterranean trade routes. The aftermath of the brutal engagement with the formidable Spanish man-of-war was painfully evident; the sails were tattered, the hull scarred, the midship destroyed, and the weary crew bore the injuries and scars of battle.

Grateful yet solemn, everyone aboard was happy to be in port alive. Merham's ship was so severely damaged that it was no longer fit to make the treacherous journey back to England. The sea had claimed its toll, and any hope of sailing home on that vessel was dashed. With quiet gratitude, the Dowlings and Captain Smith thanked Captain Merham for his courage and skill in the fight and at sea, and they parted ways.

Days passed as Peter, Margaret, and Smith waited for another ship willing to take them to England. Fortune smiled upon Smith and Dowlings when word reached them of an aged yet seasoned Captain Thomas who was in port.

After rendezvousing with Captain Thomas, the aged, weathered Captain agreed to take them aboard his sturdy vessel, promising safe passage to England. The journey was long and arduous, with rolling seas and capricious winds testing the crew's resolve. Yet, beneath the steadfast leadership of Thomas, the ship pressed on through fog and storm alike, up the English Channel, and ever closer to the familiar tributaries of the River Thames.

After several weeks at sea, the silhouette of London emerged through the morning mist, the imposing spires of the city rising proudly above the River Thames. Captain Thomas skillfully navigated his ship through the winding waterways, finally dropping anchor near the city's bustling docks. Captain Smith, Peter Dowling, and his daughter Margaret eventually stepped ashore, their hearts a mixture of relief and quiet anticipation.

All three were thrilled to be home, safe in their home country with money in their pockets. They had evaded the empires of blood that surrounded them for so long and were thankful for the sweet scents of London. They anonymously walked the streets, soaking up the town's revisions and updates. A few new cobblestone streets replace the once muddy bogs of the north shore. There was new construction everywhere, and tradespeople were hard at work on every street corner.

As they meandered through London, Peter noticed a vast crowd gathering at the Tower of London, a massive stone fortress built by William the Conqueror in the 11th Century. Its fortified stone walls were intimidating and impenetrable. Not only did the Tower of London hold the most heinous criminals of England, Ireland, and Scotland, but it also housed the priceless crown jewels.

Peter, Margaret, and Smith slung their little belongings over their shoulders and marched toward the crowd to investigate all the commotion. Peter had read that Sir Walter Raleigh, famous throughout England for his courage and the favour he received from Queen Elizabeth, was imprisoned by the new King James for treason. He thought this was the execution of Raleigh, the man who brought tobacco and potatoes to England and Europe.

Once inside the courtyard surrounding the Tower of London, they caught word from eavesdropping that this was, in fact, a public execution.

From within the tower, Guy Fawkes and his fellow conspirators were marched through the yard, tied at the wrists and ankles. They moved incredibly slowly after days of torture within the tower walls. Visual cuts and bruises were all over the sullen prisoners. The restless crowd began pelting the prisoners with rotten fruits and vegetables.

"Look!" Peter yelled over the noise of the crowd. "It's Raleigh!" he said, pointing.

"And that must be Fawkes!" Smith yelled.

Peter, Margaret, and Smith watched the men walk toward the central, elevated platform, where a black-veiled executioner stood waiting, alongside his supporting cast of helpers. There were the gallows, with five corresponding ropes, five wooden tables, and a central, raised table with all the executioner's tools.

The convicts were marched onstage to the roar of trumpets from atop the surrounding walls. The crowd came to a hush, as the executioner spoke to the crowd: "You have been drawn on a hurdle to the place of execution, where you shall be hanged by the neck and being alive cut down, your privy members shall be cut off and your bowels taken out and burned before you, your head severed from your body and your body divided into four quarters to be disposed of at the King's pleasure."

"The King's pleasure?" Peter said with a furrowed brow.

"I don't want to be here," Margaret said.

The trumpets sounded again, and King James I appeared on the royal balcony, and the crowd went completely silent. The regal James stepped forward.

"You there, Sir Walter Raleigh. Guilt surrounds you and your role within this conspiracy." There was a long, drawn-out pause.

"I can't believe they would execute Sir Walter Raleigh," Peter said. "He was England's dearest explorer and soldier."

The crowd murmured as King James raised his hand to motion silence. "I, King James, recall you, Sir Walter, into this prison and hereby save your meaningless life. As for you, Fawkes, Wintour, Rookwood, and Keyes, you will die on this day, January 31st," James said. "I shall enjoy watching you die."

"I guess Raleigh will live to see another day," Smith said to Dowling.

"He saves him to draw favour from the kingdom," Peter replied.

A pair of royal guards brought Sir Walter Raleigh back through the mob and inside the Tower of London. The crowd cheered for their hero, who helped defeat the Spanish Armada, discovered new lands, and named the new colony of Virginia after the beloved Queen Elizabeth.

"You Guy Fawkes, Thomas Wintour, Ambrose Rookwood, and Robert Keyes, after confessing your guilt before the good King James, you have been dragged here to the Old Palace Yard at Westminster. Fitting that you shall die looking at the building you had attempted to destroy," the executioner said with a loud booming voice.

The crowd watched as the conspirators were placed on the torture rack. The ragged, beaten men who once tried to have Lady Stuart claim the throne were, one by one, stretched by the neck, arms, and feet. The slow pulling of the ropes dislocated several of the men's shoulders, hips and elbows. The pops could be heard throughout the courtyard, sending shivers down the spines of the onlookers.

The ceremony carried on until the weak, helpless conspirators were marched up the steps to the gallows, where they would hang. Guy Fawkes could barely walk after days of sickness and torture. After the ropes were placed around the necks of the men, Fawkes prematurely jumped before the others. He dropped ten feet. As the rope reached the end, his neck snapped, his body went limp, and his body dangled in front of a shocked crowd.

"I don't want to watch anymore," Margaret said.

One by one, the conspirators twitched as the gallows rope stretched them. Eventually, they were each cut down, while still alive, and placed atop the various tables. The lead executioner took his sharpest 12-inch knife and, one by one, cut off the genitals of the remaining prisoners. The screams of the men echoed against the stone walls, horrifying the people of London.

The executioner then sliced open their abdomens, removed their intestines, and placed them in a small, central iron fireplace. All the men were either dead or passed out when the axe began to fall. The blood poured over the edges of the platform as the crowd grew eerily silent at the horrific nature of the spectacle. The bodies were then beheaded, quartered, and carted away, as the crowd started to disperse, including Smith and the Dowlings.

It was a gruesome ceremony that truly bothered and disgusted Margaret. "Why do they make it such a big event? Couldn't they just do that within the castle walls?" she asked.

"The mob loves violence," Captain Smith said, as they walked down the street looking for lodging for the night. "Since ancient times, blood sells tickets."

"King James, I'm certain, has reclaimed all of Raleigh's estates, including Elizabeth's gift of Virginia," Peter said.

"Well, should we grab something to eat?" Smith asked. "I'll pay!" he said, trying to shift the conversation away from the violence they had all just witnessed.

"I could go for a pint of fine English lager," Peter said. "It's been a while."

"Let's go see Miss Quickly at the Crown and Pheasant!" Margaret suggested.

"Great idea, kid," Peter said with a smile.

Chapter 35 - A Celebration of Victory

Elizabeth Bathory's lavish party was a vision of grandeur, a night woven with layers of gaiety, music, and laughter. Nobles from distant corners of Hungary, Austria, and beyond had journeyed to her castle, dressed in Asian silks and bright velvets. Each of them complimented Bathory and the servants about how clean and well-maintained the castle was.

Aromas of roasted meats and freshly baked breads filled the air as servants moved gracefully, presenting a seven-course feast, each dish more exquisite than the last. The tables groaned under the weight of delicate Italian wines, while layered pastries and exotic Asian fruits provided a sweet ending to the indulgence.

Laughter bubbled from every corner of the castle, as guests revelled in the peace finally coming to Hungary, Wallachia, and Transylvania after years of unrest. The sound of clinking glasses and the hum of cheerful conversation filled the grand stone hall. All the bloodshed and chaos had been forgotten for a few moments. The country was at peace, or so it seemed.

Despite the joy that filled the air, a shadow was quietly creeping across the land. King Matthias of Austria-Hungary, ever the shrewd tactician, had noticed the growing instability in the empire, and he was quietly making moves against his brother, Emperor Rudolph II. Soon, the winds of conflict would stir once more, but for now, the nobles were content to ignore the rumblings of war, focusing instead on the pleasures of the evening.

Even Elizabeth was enjoying the evening at first. Her dark eyes, usually sharp and calculating, softened as she observed the joy and celebration around her. She smiled faintly, nodding in approval as her guests enjoyed themselves. But beneath the surface, something far darker was brewing within her.

Her personal musician, Maria Kovacs, had fallen ill, stricken with a terrible flu that had taken her from the grand hall to the sickroom. Without Maria's delicate music filling the air, the party felt oddly incomplete to Elizabeth. Music was the lifeblood of her gatherings, the pulse that kept the festivities flowing. Without it, there was a void, a silence that gnawed at her; a sharp reminder of her growing frustration.

The Countess began to refuse to acknowledge her guests, her mind consumed with the irritation that her celebration had been so thoroughly disrupted. The laughter and conversation around her seemed muffled. People tried to speak with her, offer congratulations, and enjoy her company, but she ignored them with dismissive waves of her hand.

Her closest servants, Dorka, Illona, and Helena, were the only ones who dared approach her, but even they were met with cold silence. The Countess paid them no mind as they whispered amongst themselves, concerned for her sudden change in demeanour. Her lips were drawn tight, her gaze distant and unblinking. The flickering candlelight cast strange shadows across her face, highlighting the tension in her features.

Elizabeth's eyes narrowed, and for the first time that evening, she turned her back on her guests, retreating to her private chambers. There, in the solitude of her room, she would stew in her rage, plotting her next move. The merrymaking outside faded into the background, replaced by the sharp, oppressive silence that echoed in her mind.

—William Mowat—

—1599: Empires of Blood—

Chapter 36 - A New World Project

King James I had issued a charter for the colonization of the eastern seaboard of North America, and Captain John Smith had spent the last couple of months in London trying to organize a capable, desirable bunch of men to volunteer as colonists. The young adventurer had found his next calling.

Smith tried to find viable investors, merchants, and nobility to support the project with capital. He was more successful in finding investors than viable colonists, as most farmers, mechanics, and skilled labourers could not commit to leaving their industry in England. Most colonists who agreed to join the Virginia company were eager to escape their circumstances in England, or were broken-down gentlemen, indifferent characters, or soldiers looking for gainful employment.

Smith walked down the muddy, spring streets of London. Today, he decided to visit the Dowlings at their new home, purchased with funds from the Habsburgs. It had been a few months since their arrival home from the Carpathian Mountains, and he was excited to see old friends.

He knocked on their modest home door, and a moment later, Margaret opened it.

"Well, hello there, Captain Smith. How are you this afternoon?" she asked.

"I've never been better, Margaret. Is your father home?" Smith inquired.

Peter Dowling appeared from around the corner. "Hello there, stranger," he said. "What brings you out here? Come inside."

Smith stepped inside, knocking the mud from his boots. "Well, to get straight to the point, the King has issued a charter bound for Virginia, and I've come looking for able-bodied men to help establish a colony," Smith said, getting straight to the point, like the soldier he was.

Smith knew Peter would be the perfect colonist. He was intelligent, able to solve problems, communicated clearly, and was the ultimate team-mate and diplomat. Smith never saw Peter lose his composure and knew he would be an excellent translator for the newly encountered native people - the naturals of the New World.

"Young man, I don't think I have the energy in me. You are still incredibly young and full of ambition, " Peter said. "However, I am in no position to leave England right now, as I have commitments here, including Margaret's new business."

"I understand completely. I have been receiving many of these same responses," Smith said. "We have been looking for educated, rational men to help with farming, building, and maintenance. It seems the only interested men are retired drunk soldiers, or complete and utter buffoons."

Peter paused and sat down at his kitchen table, thinking hard about what he would say. He glanced at Margaret, then met Smith's eyes. "John, since you were a little boy, I knew you would be successful in whatever you undertook. Though grammar certainly was not your favourite subject, I knew you would be successful and could accomplish anything, if you only put your mind to it. You have been highly decorated in the military, the King obviously trusts in your abilities, and you have earned yourself a small fortune along the way. I would trust you with my life, John. Though I would never make that dangerous voyage across the Atlantic, I am certain you can and will. You could lead men into a new future who will look up to you and your leadership, Captain Smith. Establish new rights for men and new boundaries of governance; do what can't be done here. Let every man live as a king or queen. Let them control their own destinies. Set good relations with the Natives, trade with them, learn their customs, and they could be the key to success in the Americas. John, you are the perfect man for this job and will lead them to glory." Peter put his hand atop John's rough hands. "This is your calling, Captain Smith."

John smiled at his former teacher. "Thank you, Mr. Dowling. I will always cherish your words."

—William Mowat—

Chapter 37 - 1608

Emperor Rudolph made his way to the dungeons of the Royal Castle of Prague. He was slow, very deliberate in steps, and unhealthily coughing the entire way into the dungeons, as he visited his son for the first time since his horrific crime.

He once thought so highly of his son Don Julius that he gave him an entire castle with the servants and a pathway into royal servitude. Unfortunately, and gruesomely, he violently cut and beat his wife on dozens of occasions. Suffering a major delusional episode, Don thought he had killed his girlfriend, Marketa, and threw her out a window, but somehow, she survived. The Emperor's son then forced Marketa back into his bedchamber by extorting her parents to do so.

Madness convinced Don Julius to cut Marketa's body into several pieces, including beheading the poor, innocent girl. Now, Rudolph would look upon his son to see the monster he had become.

The smell was putrid. Fecal matter, urine, and body odour permeated the air of Don Julius' cell, causing Rudolph to place a handkerchief over his mouth and nose. Battling his own mental health issues, Rudolph wanted to see him one last time and try to reason with his son before dying. He sat outside Don Julius' cell and looked at his son in complete squalor, filthy and obviously refusing to bathe. He banged his head against the stone wall.

"Don Julius, it's me, your father," the saddened Emperor said. He could not believe what he had become. He longed for the time when he had been a small child, innocent and full of joy.

"Father, father, father," Don Julius repeated. "Father, father, father."

It made Rudolph's heart sink to realize his son did not recognize him.

"I will always love you, Don Julius, even if the devil possesses you." Rudolph walked back up the steps, knowing he would never see his child again.

Within a week, the ulcer Don Julius had in his stomach erupted, killing him during the night. Rudolph did not attend his funeral and fell into a deep, dark depression that isolated him for months.

While in his isolation, Rudolph was paid a visit by his brother Matthias. Rudolph reluctantly signed *The Letter of Majesty,* which he put forth. The document relinquished his capacity as King of Bohemia and granted religious freedom to Catholics and Protestants living there.

King Matthias was displeased with his shameful brother. They had grown up very close, but the brotherly feud intensified as Rudolph's health deteriorated. Now Matthias had to focus on the horrors surrounding Castle Cachtice and the ongoings of Countess Bathory.

Despite the peace in the kingdom of Hungary and a wondrous, recent celebration at Castle Cachtice, the Countess Bathory had fallen back into her routine of terror. She had been slaughtering girls daily, as Fitzko, Dorka, Helena, and Illona continued to gather them from surrounding villages. The festering smells returned, as did the uncleanliness of the castle. Elizabeth also had the young Maria imprisoned in the castle's dungeon due to her absence and exclusion from the celebration.

Maria had been handcuffed inside her cell for weeks, with only water to drink and gruel every other day. She was weak and prayed to God that her mother and father would save her. She dreamed of playing with her little brother Sam and longed to embrace Michael again. As she prayed, she promised God to live a pure, righteous life under his rule. She shed tears day and night, and found her strength and soul leaving her. Cuts and bruises were all over her body, from the handcuffs and initial beating she had taken at the hands of the Countess.

Bathory's cousin, Count George Thurzo, mulled over a goblet of wine while organizing all the evidence that he had collected surrounding the brutalities at Castle Cachtice. King Matthias had tasked him with the proceeding.

Thurzo's second wife was always by his side. Eliza and George had six children together and were devotedly in love. Eliza had grown to despise the Countess after hearing all of the stories from locals surrounding Bathory and her estates.

"More and more letters; new witnesses every day, without fail," George said to Eliza, as he shuffled through papers.

"You must act quickly, George, before hundreds more are killed beneath her scaly feet," Eliza responded.

Count Thurzo had substantial judicial and administrative authority in Hungary and had been hearing and reading dozens of extensive testimonies from witnesses and survivors. Though at the back of his mind, he was also motivated and excited by his potential takeover of the Nadasdy-Bathory estates, should Elizabeth be found guilty.

A month earlier, Thurzo had sent for direct witnesses from the village of Cachtice. He knew their information and testimony would be crucial if a conviction happened. Pastor Istivan and the Kovacs family were among those invited to Thurzo's castle, and they were ready to give their testimony regarding the disappearance of their daughter Maria and several others who had gone missing.

Thurzo's servant entered the study. "My Lord, Pastor Istivan, and the Kovacs family have arrived."

"Excellent, show them in," Thurzo responded. "And have my secretary, Attila, join us."

Eliza left the servant, and moments later, Istivan, Jan, and Catharine Kovacs entered, followed by Thurzo's secretary, Attila, a short, distinguished man with ink-stained fingertips.

"Good afternoon, Pastor Istivan. It is an honour to have you here again," Thurzo began. "This is my secretary, Attila. He will be recording and documenting your testimonies," he said as Attila began removing his ink and quills from his small wooden box.

"Thank you, my Lord, for allowing us to bring our cases before you," Istivan said. "Your Highness, this is Catharine and Jan Kovacs, from the Village of Cachtice. They, too, have lost a daughter in the confines of the Bathory court."

Jan and Catharine bowed and smiled at Thurzo.

"Thank you for coming, Mr. and Mrs. Kovacs. I have been documenting dozens of accounts these past months, and found plenty of evidence of her guilt. What is your story, exactly?" Thurzo asked.

Without hesitation, Jan began: "Our daughter has been playing music at the Pastor's sermons for years, and Elizabeth Bathory took a fancy to her abilities and invited her to formal courtly education at her gynaeceum. A small, deformed evil dwarf picked her up, and we have not heard a word since," Jan said.

"She promised to write and visit us ever so often, but she has been vacant and absent from all correspondence, which is completely unlike her," Catharine added. "Please help us, my Lord."

"Our daughter means everything to us. She is the light that brightens our world," Jan said. "That evil devil has taken her from us."

"Describe this dwarf servant," Thurzo asked.

"A mean, nasty, deformed little man. Knotty, untidy hair, gnarled lip, haunch in his shoulders," Catharine answered.

"I have heard many stories of this man-servant. It seems he is always the driver of the kidnappings. Always promises of wealth and noble marriage," Thurzo responded.

"The funerals continue as well, my Lord," Istivan intervened. "Dozens, week by week, always closed caskets. We need only dig up one of these caskets to show the evil doings of the Countess."

"I hope it does not come to that, Pastor," Thurzo said grimly.

Attila wrote frantically to capture every word said by the Kovacs and Istivan. Thurzo continued asking questions about the timelines of Maria's departure and other girls they knew about. Near the end of the interview, Thurzo put down everything, removed his hat, and stared at Pastor Istivan and the Kovacs.

"The good people of our kingdom, brothers and sisters, mothers and fathers, have all come forth with their testimonies. Now I, the Palatine of Hungary, and father myself, must guard the sons and daughters of our kingdom," Thurzo said. "So we may finally end this devilish work, I ask you to accompany me to Castle Cachtice on the morrow, so that we may apprehend Countess Bathory and her evil servants."

Maria watched on from a neighbouring cell as Elizabeth burned another teenage girl with red-hot iron spikes all over her innocent body. The harrowing screams echoed throughout the castle dungeon. The burns, shaped like lashings, had begun to swell and pus from head to toe.

Elizabeth was meticulous with her torture techniques. She would keep the girls alive as long as possible and get as much entertainment as possible out of each life. She would deliberately wait and watch the girl, as Fitzko reheated the iron spikes.

Maria could do nothing but cry in silence at the horrific sight of the unspeakable cruelties happening around her.

Count Thurzo stood in front of two dozen armed horsemen, Pastor Istivan, Catharine, and Jan Kovacs at the front gates of his castle. "I have heard your cries; your whispers carried on winds of sorrow and fear. Too many of our children with unwritten futures have vanished behind Castle Cachtice's walls. We have waited, prayed, wept, and shall no longer wait. You, loyal subjects and fellow soldiers, our kingdom speaks of cruelty, bloodshed, and of a noblewoman whose thirst for darkness defies the laws of God and man alike. Countess

Bathory will no longer hide behind title, wealth, and nobility. We ride now, not as a guest, but as an agent of justice. Her reign ends today."

Thurzo turned his horse about, and the riders departed along the Carpathian road toward Castle Cachtice.

Elizabeth spoke to the burned, bleeding girl on the dungeon floor: "Hush now, girl. Don't waste your breath on screams. Each cry is a song I have heard, and none of them has saved a soul. I have walked for decades, untouched and adored, and while peasants rot in fields, I remain the Countess Bathory. Your blood, your warmth, your terror nourishes more than you know. It feeds something greater than you. Something eternal." Elizabeth moved to the small iron fireplace. "My dear, the world worships monsters draped in silk, so long as they smile and are victorious. Soon, the pain will be numb. Your eyes will grow distant and vacant. And you will become part of something timeless. Is that not better than being forgotten in some cold village, buried nameless in the mud?"

Maria could not believe the sheer insanity of the Countess. Her delusional grandeur was revolting. She envisioned herself cutting the Countess's head off.

Elizabeth spun her head towards Maria, who cowered in the corner of her cell. "Don't think I have forgotten about you, Maria, and your indifference."

After a long and exhausting ride, George Thurzo and his riders approached the mountain leading to Castle Cachtice. "We shall search every chamber, question every accomplice, and turn every stone. If your child still breathes, I will not rest until she is returned to your arms," Thurzo said to Jan and Catharine.

"Finally, justice has come to Cachtice!" Pastor Istivan yelled. "May God grant us strength, and may He watch over the innocent."

The girl whom Elizabeth had been burning was now dead on the floor with her neck slit open. Elizabeth rubbed the girl's blood into her cheeks as she approached Maria in the neighbouring cell.

"Sing me something pretty," Elizabeth said.

Maria composed herself and sang a verse from Elizabeth's favourite song:

Beneath the silver moon's soft light,
Where roses blush and stars take flight,
I wait for thee, my heart's delight,
In the moonlit garden's tender night.

"Ah, lovely, keep going," Elizabeth demanded.
Maria continued:

Oh, walk with me, through fields of green,
Where only love and dreams are seen,
And in the hush of night's embrace,
We find our hearts, our hearts' true place.

Elizabeth dreamed of Ferenc and their children frolicking in the Cachtice wheat fields. A smile came to her face, but the memory was shattered by Fitzko barging through the dungeon doors.

She immediately resumed her evil intentions as she snapped out of her memory. "Watch carefully, Fitzko. Witness the most gifted singer in all of Europe's tongue fall to the floor," Elizabeth said. "Stick your tongue out, Maria."

Maria reluctantly stuck out her tongue as Elizabeth pulled a dagger from her dress.

"My Lady, I hate to interrupt, but your cousin, Count Thurzo, has arrived. He has ordered that he be admitted at once," Fitzko said.

"Have you allowed him in?" asked Elizabeth.

"I had no choice. He has come with armoured soldiers on horseback, your Grace."

"You deformed, ugly idiot. Find Dorka, Helena, and Illona, and find out what my cousin wants. I will be along in a moment." Elizabeth turned to Maria, once again. "Finally, some peace and quiet. Now, let us see that sweet tongue again, my dear."

Maria, again, reluctantly stuck out her tongue for the Countess. As soon as Elizabeth brought the dagger up to make the incision, Count Thurzo burst through the door with two of his guards.

"Restrain her!" Thurzo ordered his guards.

"You shall pay for this intrusion, cousin," Elizabeth said as two guards grabbed her by the arms.

"Not so, my lady. The misdeeds of this castle are finished. Arrest that dwarf!" Thurzo said, pointing at Fitzko.

"No one is to interrupt my work," Elizabeth said, struggling against the guards.

"Your work is over, cousin. Let the courts of justice determine your fate. Shadows will surround you for as long as you live to repent of this bestial life, Mistress of Cachtice."

"Hear my words, cousin, I am Elizabeth Bathory, royalty to this country. I shall be free before you leave this castle."

"The good King Matthias and I have reason to believe otherwise, your Grace," Thurzo said with a smile.

The guards removed Bathory and Fitzko as Thurzo approached the barely conscious Maria.

"Child, can you hear me? You are safe now. My name is George Thurzo. I have come to end this nightmare. Look at me, my dear. I am here. There is light now. There is hope." Thurzo unshackled Maria, and she collapsed in his arms. "They told us rumours, whispers of horror, but I did not imagine this," he said, looking around at the piles of bodies and blood-stained cells. "The devil herself will harm you no more. Her reign is finished."

Chapter 38 - Return Home

Jan and Catharine were thrilled to have their daughter back after the significant trauma she had endured. Maria spent the following weeks in bed, being nourished back to health by her parents and loyal friend, Michael. Her wrists were severely cut and bruised, and she was malnourished and weak, to the point where she could not stand.

Day after day, Maria's strength returned, and she began to process everything she had been through. She had been having terrible nightmares, soaked in terror and sweat. Vivid dreams of being burned alive and being hanged by the neck. In one particular dream, her fingers were cut off, and blood splashed all over the church organ and altar, with the bodies of dead girls spread throughout the pews and aisles of the holy place.

Maria slept most days and nights as her wounds healed. Michael did not leave her side; he gently washed her wounds, gave her water, fed her spoonfuls of food, and read the Bible as she lay recovering. He just wished he could have done something more proactive or heroic earlier. Though he did report his findings to Pastor Istivan, who reported them to Count George Thurzo, it did not seem enough.

Maria's little brother Sam was happy to see his sister again, though he was confused by the situation.

Pastor Istivan knocked on the door of the Kovacs home in the early afternoon, and Catharine opened the door. Without hesitation, she embraced the shy Pastor, who flushed red.

"Thank you for saving our daughter," Catharine said, as she shed a tear on the shoulder of his robe.

Pastor Istivan felt a small sense of accomplishment as he realized how important Maria was to her family and the entire community. He had collected hundreds of signatures and reports damning Bathory and her servants, and now his hard work and persistence were paying off.

"I am so happy that Maria has returned home. How has she been feeling?" Istivan asked.

"She is recovering slowly, Father," Catharine responded.

From around the bedroom corner, a weak, pale Maria appeared. She took slow steps towards Pastor Istivan and gave a very faint smile.

"There is our brave girl," Istivan said.

"Hello, Father," Maria softly said.

"It brings great joy to my heart to see you feeling better, my dear. You have endured so much over these past months. When you feel ready and able, please come back to our congregation. We have missed your angelic voice and talent." Father gave her a gentle hug and smiled.

"Thank you for everything you have done, Father. I was so close to death. I felt entirely helpless there. The devil stirred in every corner of her castle, rats, bugs, vermin everywhere. The smells, Father; death, rotten, nauseating death. Hundreds of bodies, some buried, some fed to the wolves, some burned, and others left to decompose by the bugs and worms. The servants of the castle were always watching, always ready to enslave and kill, Father. I hope the Countess and her minions are punished with the harshest arm of the law in all reason and justice."

"They will be punished, my dear," Istivan assured.

—William Mowat—

Chapter 39 - The Trial

Thurzo had a letter written for his wife, Eliza, while he continued to deal with the aftermath of the Bathory killings:

My Beloved Heart,
I arrived here yesterday evening in good health, thank God. I apprehended the Bathory woman. By now, she has been led away to the castle tower. Now, those who tortured and murdered the innocent - those evil women in league with that young dwarf who, in silent cruelty, assisted them with their atrocities were sent to prison. They are under guard and will be held in strict captivity until, God willing, I arrive home to bring the substantial justice they deserve. The women can remain imprisoned in the town, but the young lad must be confined at the castle.
As for our people and servants I brought with me, when my men entered Cachtice, they found a girl dead in the house; another followed in death as a result of many wounds and agonies. In addition to this, there was also a wounded

and tortured woman there; the other victims were kept hidden away, where this damned woman prepared these future martyrs.

I am just waiting until this cursed woman is brought to the castle and the other's destination is determined, and then I break away and hope, if the way permits, that I make it home by tomorrow. May God grant it! I have written this in the greatest haste.

Your loving Lord and spouse,
Count George Thurzo

Bathory's four servants, Dorka, Helena, Illona, and Fitzko, were eventually captured and transported to the dungeon of the Capital Courthouse, a grim and imposing structure along the Danube River's banks. Upon arrival, it was evident that they had endured severe physical abuse; each one bore the marks of brutal beatings and appeared to be in a state of profound physical and mental deterioration. The torture they faced was not a brief ordeal but a prolonged and methodical campaign aimed at extracting confessions and information. Count Thurzo, determined to uncover all the truths behind the atrocities, assigned his own men, loyal guards skilled in coercion and intimidation, to oversee the interrogations. Under his authority, the servants were subjected to relentless questioning and further torment, their bodies and minds pushed to the breaking point in the pursuit of justice, or perhaps vengeance.

Thurzo and his team awoke the servants with the intention of beginning the next round of torture.

"This is your last day before your trial," Thurzo said. "Today will be your final chance to admit the truth about your Countess Bathory."

"We were just following orders from our Governess," Fitzko said with a lisp. "It was she who killed the girls. She bathed in their blood."

Thurzo recognized the naivety of Fitzko and the lack of intelligence, which gave rise to Thurzo's sympathy level. "You all have murdered in the first degree! What say you!" Thurzo yelled.

"We were ordered to capture girls. We did what we were told," Dorka said.

"How many girls were there?" Thurzo asked.

"Twenty, maybe thirty," Helena answered.

"I have over 300 reports from surrounding families across Hungary. These numbers are not adding up."

"It may have been that many; we only buried the bodies, we didn't do the killing," Illona pleaded.

"Tomorrow will be your trial. Prepare for your death," Thurzo impatiently said.

The next day, the cold, damp air of the courtroom hung heavy with anticipation. The high vaulted ceilings of the court were covered in the flickering light of torches, as Elizabeth Bathory's four servants were brought to the raised platform at the centre of the room.

Elizabeth Bathory was left imprisoned at Castle Cachtice until a punishment was issued. As a Countess, she was refrained from trial and prosecution. King Matthias understood she could never be executed, so she was separated from her servants' trial and the public mob.

In front of a large crowd at the courthouse, George Thurzo began the litany of accusations against Bathory and her servants. Hundreds of witnesses were gathered to testify regarding the Countess and her servants. From priests to nobles, to farmers and doctors, the citizens of Hungary were determined to rid their kingdom of devilry.

"Hundreds of reports of murder, torture, and the vile claim of bathing in the blood of young virgin girls," Thurzo said, shaking his head in disgust. "Several testimonies of flesh being cut from virgin girls, cooked, and then forced to consume their own body." Behind him, dozens of witnesses sat in silence, looking at the Countess's evil servants in their vulnerable state, and listening to the grim reports from Count Thurzo.

Each witness confessed their vivid, grim story of the Countess's evildoings. First-hand accounts of missing daughters, sisters, cousins, stories of seeing mutilated bodies, tortured souls, and improper burials all over the Hungarian landscape. Even for the desensitized, it was a disturbing trial.

Nearing the end of the day, Dorka, Illona, Helena, and Fitzko were finally brought in as witnesses and were forced to testify under the duress of torture against Bathory. Throughout the trial, they did everything they could to plead their innocence and pin the guilt on their Countess.

"What say you, Illona, to these heinous crimes of murder, betrayal, and sabotage?" Thurzo asked. "What say you against all these first-hand accounts?"

The room grew quiet. Her lips pressed into a thin line, her posture regal despite the chains that bound her. She glanced around the massive courtroom. "You speak of blood and torture, but you have not seen what I have seen. You do not understand the burden I carry for this kingdom, the weight upon my shoulders." Illona then paused, and an almost contemptuous smile came across her face. "Do you not see? What I did was necessary, for your survival, for the survival of the kingdom."

Her words unsettled the court, as most sneered at her delusional arrogance and failure to understand the gravity of the horrific crimes.

Account after account, Thurzo read, graphic detail after graphic detail. Stories of rotten burials, biting chunks of flesh, more girls forced to eat their own flesh, cooked and uncooked. As the trial continued, the true horror was vividly exposed. The nightmares that had taken place within the walls of her castles would not be easily forgotten.

Even Fitzko began to expose the details. "Besides the bodies we burned inside the castle, five bodies were tossed into a pit; two into the water canal in the Cachtice garden, one of which was dragged out by the dogs; two brought at night to Lesticze and buried at the church; these were brought down from the castle where they had been murdered," Fitzko said as he pointed to Dorka. "The old woman hid and buried the dead girls. At Cachtice, I buried a dozen, two at Lesticze, one at Keresztur, one at Sarvar, and others were buried with regular funeral rites." It seemed Fitzko had lost count of how many bodies there actually were.

The weight of guilt surrounding the Countess and her loyal servants was palpable, suffocating even, and it did not go unnoticed by Thurzo or the court members. From the outset, the sheer volume of damning evidence painted a chilling portrait of cruelty and bloodshed. Yet, despite the clarity of the case, Thurzo methodically continued to summon witness after witness, each testimony peeling back another layer of horror. Survivor accounts, confessions, and firsthand observations converged into a damning chorus of voices that left no room for potential innocence. Every new revelation only deepened the court's revulsion and solidified the already inescapable truth: Countess Elizabeth Bathory's guilt was beyond question. The trial, though thorough, seemed more a grim formality than a pursuit of justice. The outcome was a foregone conclusion etched into the horrified expressions of all who heard the accounts of her monstrous deeds.

Several days after the damning conclusion of the trial, outside the grand Hungarian courthouse, a wooden platform had been hastily erected. At its centre stood a tall, weathered, and splintered post, now serving as the final pillar of judgment for the Countess's most devoted accomplices.

Dorka, Ilona, and Helena, stripped of their former arrogance and now clad in soiled, tattered garments, were each led to the platform under heavy guard. Their faces bore expressions of fear and resignation; a grotesque reflection of the horrors they had helped inflict. Their arms were tightly bound with coarse rope to the central post, the wood biting into their skin as guards secured them in place. Around the platform's base, bundles of dry straw and hay were carefully arranged, mingled with kindling sticks and thick pine logs.

A small but restless crowd had gathered, murmuring with anticipation and unease, some drawn by morbid curiosity, others seeking closure for the atrocities that had haunted the region.

Nearby, Fitzko was not bound to the platform. Instead, he stood a short distance away, his wrists shackled with iron cuffs. Two armed guards flanked him closely, their hands never far from the hilts of their swords. Though spared the torture and pain of the flames, Fitzko's fate was to witness the execution of his companions before meeting judgment in his own grim fashion.

The executioner finally appeared with a long pair of iron shears. A crowd gathered in the courtyard to watch the execution. One at a time, the cloaked executioner cut off the fingers of Dorka, Illona, and Helena. The screams of Dorka, Helena, and Illona echoed throughout the courtyard and across the mighty Danube River.

"The people have spoken, you have been sentenced to death, by order of the King. You will burn until you are dead and gone from this earth forever. Witches of Cachtice, now you die and return to where you came." His apprentice handed the executioner a torch and lit the straw bundle below the wooden platform.

Before long, Dorka, Illona, and Helena were screaming as the fire crept through the wooden sticks and logs, and up their clothing. As their clothes burned off, so did the hair on their heads. Skin began to blister and peel, as their eyes became swollen shut, and the screaming eventually stopped. The crowd could only watch in stunned silence as all three women's heads dropped and became unrecognizable as their bodies charred in the raging inferno.

Soon after the burning of Elizabeth's servants, Fitzko was brought in front of the smouldering fire and his head placed on top of a wooden barrel. The executioner grabbed his sharpened axe and approached the crouched dwarf.

"By order of the King, you are sentenced to death. Do you have any last words?" the executioner asked.

"I did my job, and I did it well. I was always told I was doing God's work. The devil has deceived me, and I repent all my sins, in the name of the Holy Father," Fitzko said as he began to cry.

—William Mowat—

The executioner's axe came down upon Fitzko's head, and it rolled amongst the smoky aftermath of the execution fire, and his small, limp body fell to the ground.

Chapter 40 - Confrontation

Fearing Elizabeth Bathory might commit suicide, two stone masons, Count Thurzo, Pastor Istivan, and a handful of other priests and guards were asked to accompany Thurzo to dissuade her from doing anything irrational before the verdict and punishment could be applied.

Countess Bathory was to be walled into a small cell, with only a small opening for food and a waste bucket. There would only be one tiny window in her cell, her only connection to the natural world. She would never see her children again; only written correspondence was permitted.

Elizabeth saw the entourage of Thurzo and his company of priests approach the tower cell where she was currently confined. She was furious at seeing them as she rose to her feet. "This is all your fault," she said, screaming at Pastor Istivan.

"It's over, Bathory," Thurzo said. "We have heard the testimony and first-hand accounts of a hundred witnesses. We caught you with dead and dying girls throughout your castle. The Kingdom of Hungary has determined a verdict."

"What verdict is that?" Elizabeth scoffed.

"You have been found guilty of murders between 1590 and 1610," Thurzo responded.

"You do not treat me right," Elizabeth said directly to Istivan. "You have angered me, and soon you will pay."

"I do not wish to anger you, Elizabeth. I am here to ask God for salvation. Kindly accept this call to repentance and partake in our Holy Communion," Istivan responded.

"I cannot partake with you as my enemies," Elizabeth said.

"Your servants, your old women, and Fitzko have confessed to their guilt and yours," Thurzo said.

"They are the guilty ones! Those damned old women," Elizabeth was enraged.

"Why then did you allow them to kill those hundreds of girls?" Thurzo asked.

"Because I was afraid of those old women. Sorcery and witchcraft," Elizabeth pleaded.

Thurzo shook his head at the lying Countess and her insincere deniability. "By order of the King and the Court of Hungary, you are ordered to be confined within these walls for the rest of your life," George Thurzo said, pointing to the masons hard at work. "These brick walls will ensure your devilish ways will never be allowed to see the light of day again. The families of the hundreds you have murdered feel secure and satisfied that you will be a forever prisoner in your own castle. May you rot within these walls," Thurzo said.

Elizabeth suddenly changed her demeanour, switching from anger to innocence. "Promise to take care of my family. They are innocent and deserve not the trials and tribulations of my legacy. Treat them fair, allow them a chance, cousin," Elizabeth said.

"I shall do my best," Thurzo said as he walked away from Elizabeth's cell.

"Promise me!" Elizabeth screamed.

"Your estates have been divided amongst your children, but they shall never rule in your name," Thurzo said. "They will be exiled."

"Take care of my children, cousin!" Elizabeth broke down in tears and slumped in defeat.

"May God have mercy on your soul," Pastor Istivan said, as everyone left, except the masons who continued to work until later that evening, when Elizabeth was transferred into her new cell and the last brick was mortared into place.

—William Mowat—

—1599: Empires of Blood—

Chapter 41 - The Tempest

Margaret and Peter Dowling, once again, were visiting the Globe Theatre for the premiere of The Tempest. The weather was cool and breezy as the crowd piled into the space. King James was also in attendance. The King loved Shakespeare and the arts and supported many of the artists within his realm.

William Shakespeare emerged from backstage with a twinkle in his eye. He had aged some since the last time Peter and Margaret had seen him, ten years ago. While Peter and Margaret were in Hungary, Shakespeare had released Twelfth Night, Othello, King Lear, Macbeth, and Hamlet, all major successes. Shakespeare was at the height of fame, and there was not a single space in the Globe.

> *Good gentles all, I bid thee hush and hearken near,*
> *For I bring forth a tale of marvels clear.*
> *From the sea's wide embrace to the winds' cruel might,*
> *A world of spirits, shipwrecks, and strange delight.*
> *This evening's play, though set in storm's cruel roar,*
> *Shall guide thee through a wondrous distant shore.*
> *A storm there shall be, and tempests wild,*
> *Yet in the storm's heart, a child's sweet smile.*
> *Come, witness all this wonder and mirth,*

As we spin this tale of magic and rebirth.

Shakespeare took a moment, looked out across the crowd, and caught the eye of Margaret staring back at him.

So stay your doubts, and let the play unfold,
For in this tempest, great truths will be told.
Now, let the stage be set and the players take their place,
And in the hands of fate, let us trust this race.

With a bow, Shakespeare winked at Margaret and stepped back. His words and character faded backstage, as the eager hum of the crowd filled the theatre.

"Good God, he is terrific," Peter said.

The play began, and Peter and Margaret could not help but notice the parallels between Prospero and Miranda and themselves. The characters were loyal, naive, protective, and loving.

After the three-hour magical performance, Peter and Margaret made the long walk home. Initially, they spoke of Shakespeare's themes and characters, then shifted to the comfortable silence they often shared. As she frequently did, Margaret reflected on their journey to Castle Cachtice. The trauma had caused her severe grief; however, over the past couple of years, scars had healed, and she found meaningful work in London. When the news of Elizabeth Bathory's imprisonment arrived in London, she felt a massive load lift from her shoulders.

Peter had also endured a long recovery, having witnessed so many horrific things at the hands of the Countess. He had learned valuable lessons and promised never to endanger himself or his daughter again. Peter's money allowed him to buy a lovely house and create a dowry for Margaret.

As they strolled down the cobblestone streets, they could not help but be thankful for all they had. The Dowlings turned onto their street and finally arrived home to find a man sitting on their front step. The man appeared ragged and grim, with a bandage around his arm that rested in a sling. He leaned on a wooden crutch and smoked a pipe, his head bowed as he stared down at his feet.

The man slowly lifted his head at the newly arrived Peter and Margaret.

"Captain Smith!" Margaret yelled.

The once vibrant, young soldier looked visibly older. His eyes had sunken, and grey hairs appeared on his head and face. He struggled to get to his feet as soon as he noticed the arrival of Peter and Margaret.

"Captain Smith, it has been too long," Peter said. "I thought you had made the trip to Virginia?"

"Well, Mr. Dowling, I returned from Virginia a while back and thought I would come by for a visit," Smith said. "It has been too long."

"By God, across the ocean and back again. I heard there were some struggles in Virginia, but all is sorted now, since the reinforcement of Jamestown," Peter said. "How are you? Are you injured? I have so many questions," Peter said.

"What happened to your arm, Captain Smith?" Margaret asked.

"Unfortunately, I had a gunpowder accident a few months back. But other than that, I am doing just fine," Smith said, smiling at Margaret. "After a terrible first year in America, we have successfully established colonies in Virginia, though not exactly easily. Quite grim, establishing our relations with the natives, some long stories I would love to share, if you have the time," he said.

"We have not heard much of Virginia, here in London, just the initial struggles and recent successes in establishing Jamestown," Peter said.

"You must have exciting stories of Powhatan, Pocohontas, and the natives," Margaret said.

"My two long years in Virginia were cobbled with starvation, disease, cannibalism, and violence, almost as gruesome as the battlefields of eastern Europe," Smith said with a cheeky smile.

"I could not imagine two months at sea," Margaret said.

"That was the easy part," Smith said. "The hard part was dealing with the first crew that set sail to Jamestown. If we had some educated diplomats and orderly governance, things might have gone a lot differently."

"You should write a book about your adventures!" Margaret exclaimed.

"Come inside, Captain," Peter said. "Let's get reacquainted and tell me more about your days in America."

On their way up the step, Smith turned to Peter. "Tell me, whatever happened to the Countess Bathory?" he asked.

"Let's get a cup of tea, and I will tell you all about it," Peter said, putting his arm around the shoulder of Captain Smith.

Epilogue

The cold stone walls of Castle Cachtice stood in silence as the days turned into weeks, then months. Time seemed to stretch endlessly within the brick cell where Elizabeth Bathory had been confined. The once-proud Countess, a figure of terrifying power, now spent her days in darkness, her mind slowly unravelling in the shadow of her confinement.

Within the dim confines of her cell, Elizabeth had long since lost track of the days. Her face, gaunt and pale, reflected the inner decay of her soul. She would no longer stand before courts; her royal name was no longer held in high esteem in Hungary. As the years passed, she could only face the bitter truth that her immortality had been a lie, that her power had been nothing more than a fragile illusion.

She sat alone in the darkness of her cell, her thoughts a twisted maze of regret, defiance, and madness. The world had taken its revenge.

Elizabeth Bathory died one evening, and not long after, her assets were passed on to her children, who were exiled to Poland-Lithuania. Her castles and lands were forfeited, and her name was no longer associated with royalty and nobility.

—William Mowat—

Bibliography

Bolton, Henry C. *The Follies of Science at the Court of Rudolph (1576-1612)*. Pharmaceutical Review Publishing Co. 1904.

Brotton, Jerry. *The Renaissance Bazaar: From the Silk Road to Michelangelo.* Oxford University Press, 2002.

Charles River Editors. *Countess Elizabeth Bathory: The Life and Legacy of History's Most Prolific Female Serial Killer*. Amazon Digital Services / KDP, 2017.

Craft, Kimberly L. *Infamous Lady: The True Story of Countess Erzsébet Báthory.* 2nd Edition 2014. CreateSpace Independent Publishing Platform.

Craft, Kimberly L. *The Private Letters of Countess Erzsébet Báthory.* CreateSpace Independent Publishing Platform, 2011.

Evans, R. J. W. *Rudolf II and His World: A Study in Intellectual History, 1576–1612.* Oxford University Press, 1973.

Jenks, Tudor. *Captain John Smith.* New York: The Century Co., 1904.

Johnson, Rossiter. *Captain John Smith (1579-1631).* New York: The Macmillan Company, 1915.
The Library of Congress

Marshall, Peter. *The Magic Circle of Rudolf II: Alchemy and Astrology in Renaissance Prague.* Walker & Company, 2006.

McNally, Raymond T. *Dracula Was a Woman: In Search of the Blood Countess of Transylvania.* New York: McGraw-Hill, 1983.

Smith, John. *A True Relation of Such Occurrences and Accidents of Note as Hath Happened in Virginia.* London, 1608.

Smith, John. *The Generall Historie of Virginia, New-England, and the Summer Isles.* London, 1624.

Smith, John. *A Description of New England, or, Observations and Discoveries in the North of America in the Year of Our Lord 1614.* London, 1616.

Thorne, Tony. *Countess Dracula: The Life and Times of Elisabeth Bathory, the Blood Countess.* London: Bloomsbury, 1997 (later editions).

Warner, Charles Dudley. *Captain John Smith.* (Late 19th / early 20th century publication.)
Project Gutenberg

1599: Empires of Blood

—William Mowat—

www.ingramcontent.com/pod-product-compliance
Lightning Source LLC
Chambersburg PA
CBHW022203090526
44583CB00012BA/256